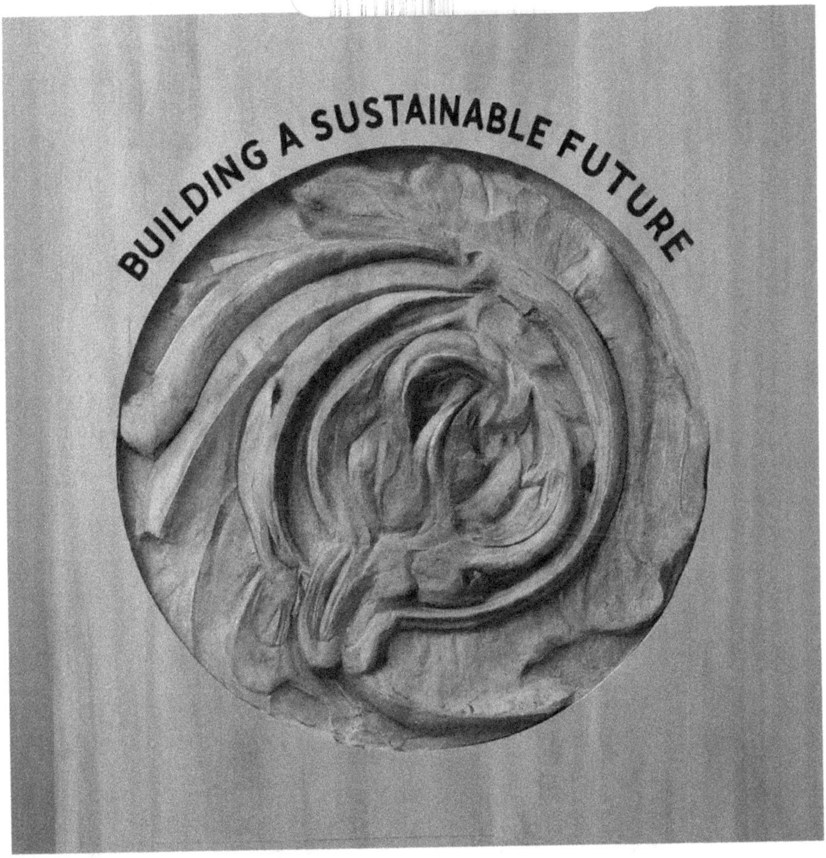

Building a Sustainable Future with Woodcraft
"A Guide to Eco-Friendly Woodworking"

-Ramesh Chauhan

PREFACE

In this rapidly changing world, the need for sustainability has never been more pressing. "Building a Sustainable Future with Woodcraft" is my contribution to this cause. As a woodworker and environmental advocate, I believe that woodworking is not just a craft but a pathway to a more sustainable lifestyle. This book is for anyone who loves working with wood and cares about the environment. Whether you are an experienced artisan or a beginner, my hope is that this guide will inspire you to adopt eco-friendly practices in your woodworking journey.

Introduction

Woodcraft has been an essential part of human civilization for millennia. Yet, in the 21st century, the craft faces new challenges and opportunities. This book explores the intersection of traditional woodworking and modern sustainability practices. Through this guide, I aim to demonstrate how woodworking can be both a creative outlet and a means of promoting environmental stewardship. Let us embark on this journey to build a sustainable future, one project at a time.

Table of contents

Introduction 5

Section 1: Introduction.. 15

Chapter 1: Why Woodcraft Matters in the 21st Century . 17

    Why Woodcraft Matters in the 21st Century 18

    The Environmental Impact of Woodworking............. 20

    The Benefits of Using Sustainable Wood 21

    Woodcraft's Role in Building a more Sustainable Future 23

    Future Challenges of Wood Art 24

    Overcoming Challenges 26

Chapter 2: The Environmental Impact of Woodworking 28

    Can Woodworking Affect the Environment?............. 28

    Measures to reduce the environmental impact of woodworking: 31

    Mitigating the Environmental Impact of Woodworking for a Sustainable Future 33

Chapter 3: Understanding Sustainable Wood Sourcing 35

The Importance of Responsible Wood Sourcing in Woodworking 36

Create a more Sustainable Future 37

The Concept of Sustainable Wood Sourcing 39

The Importance of Sourcing Wood Responsibly 41

The Importance of Forest Certification in Sustainable Wood Sourcing 42

Sustainable Wood Choices: Understanding the Pros and Cons of Different Types of Wood 44

Ethical and Social Considerations in Wood Sourcing 46

    The Impact of Unethical Practices: 46

    Fair Labor Practices: 46

    Rights of Indigenous Communities: 47

Section 2: Building a Sustainable Woodshop 49

Chapter 4:

Green Woodworking Tools and Equipment 51

    The Concept of Green Woodworking 51

    The different types of tools and equipment 52

        Hand tools 53

        Power tools 55

    The pros and cons of various options 57

Chapter 5:

Creating an Eco-Friendly Woodworking Space 59

    Creating an Eco-Friendly Woodworking Space........60

    Practical Tips for Reducing Environmental Impact...62

    The principles of eco-friendly woodworking 64

    Creating an Eco-Friendly Woodworking Space Impact 67

Chapter 6: Tips for Reducing Waste and Recycling in Your Shop 71

    The Various Ways in which Woodworkers Can Reduce Waste.. 72

    The Importance of Reducing Waste 73

    Practical Tips for Recycling Materials 75

    The Benefits of Upcycling and Repurposing Materials 77

Section 3: Eco-Friendly Woodworking Techniques..... 79

    Chapter 7: Understanding Wood Joinery and Adhesives 81

        Introduction to wood joinery and adhesives 81

        Traditional wood joinery techniques: 83

        Modern wood joinery techniques:............................ 84

        Types of wood adhesives: 85

Strength and durability of wood joints: 87

Importance of proper application: 88

Sustainability considerations: 89

    Environmental impact of traditional and modern joinery techniques: 90

    Choosing sustainable wood adhesives: 90

    Reducing waste in joinery and adhesive application: 90

    Choosing sustainably sourced wood: 90

    Consideration of product end-of-life: 91

Tips and tricks for successful joinery and adhesive application: 91

The Various Techniques and Methods 92

Chapter 8: Finishing Wood with Natural Products 95

The Various Techniques and Methods of Finishing Wood 95

    Benefits and Drawbacks 97

The best practices for achieving a smooth and durable finish 98

Chapter 9: Working with Salvaged and Reclaimed Wood 101

Salvaged and Reclaimed Wood 101

The Benefits of Working with Salvaged and Reclaimed Wood 102

The Challenges of Working with Salvaged and Reclaimed Wood..................103

The best Practices for Working with Salvaged and Reclaimed Wood..................104

Some Practical Tips and Techniques 105

Section 4: Sustainable Wood Projects............109

Chapter 10: The Different Kinds and Forms of wood crafts 111

Kinds and Forms of Woodworking............111

Carpentry............113

Cabinetry............115

Woodturning............116

Wood carving............117

Wood burning............118

Scroll sawing............119

Marquetry............120

Intarsia............121

Woodworking for construction............122

Woodworking for art and decoration............123

Chapter 11: Building Furniture with a Sustainable Mindset............125

The Ways in which Woodworkers can Build Furniture 125

The Art of Creating Handmade Wooden Furniture .129

The Techniques and Tools needed to Craft Wooden Furniture..131

The most Popular Types of Wood for Furniture......133

Chapter 12: Crafting Wooden Utensils and Kitchenware 135

The Art of Creating Handmade Wooden Utensils and Kitchenware 136

The Techniques and Tools needed to Craft Wooden Utensils and Kitchenware 137

The most Popular Types of Wood for utensils and kitchenware 139

Chapter 13: Sustainable Woodworking for Home Improvement Projects..143

The Concept of Sustainable Woodworking for Home Improvement Projects 144

The Benefits of Sustainable Woodworking 147

The Various Certification Systems.........................149

Practical Guidance on how to Incorporate Sustainable Woodworking Practices into Home Improvement Projects 151

The use of Eco-Friendly Finishes and other Sustainable Techniques..155

Section 5: The Future of Woodcraft 157

Chapter 14 : Innovations in Sustainable Woodworking according 159

   The Latest Innovations in Sustainable Woodworking 159

   How They are Shaping the Future of Woodcraft 161

   The Cutting-edge Developments 162

   The Boundaries of what is Possible in Sustainable Woodworking 164

   The Exciting Future of this Important Craft 165

Chapter 15: The Intersection of Woodworking and Technology 167

   The Intersection of Woodworking and Technology . 168

   The Latest Developments in This Field 169

   How They are Shaping the Future of Woodcraft 171

   The Potential Drawbacks of Relying too Heavily on Technology in Woodworking 172

   The intersection of woodworking and technology is a fascinating and rapidly evolving field 173

Chapter 16 175

The Role of Woodcraft in Building a Sustainable Future 175

The Role of Traditional Crafts in this Transformation 175

The Ways in which Woodcraft can Contribute to Building a more Sustainable Future 177

The many Ways in which Woodcraft can Play a Crucial Role in Sustainable Development 178

The Exciting Possibilities of this Important Craft 180

Conclusion 183

Chapter 17: Taking Action: How to Build a Sustainable Future with Woodcraft 185

Some Practical Guidance 185

The Steps You can take to Make a Positive Impact 187

The Importance of Collaboration and Community Involvement 188

Section 1: Introduction

- Chapter 1: Why Woodcraft Matters in the 21st Century
- Chapter 2: The Environmental Impact of Woodworking
- Chapter 3: Understanding Sustainable Wood Sourcing

Chapter 1:

Why Woodcraft Matters in the 21st Century

As we enter the 21st century, our society is becoming increasingly aware of the impact we have on the environment. From the food we eat to the products we use, there is a growing recognition that our choices have consequences. As a result, many people are turning to sustainable practices, seeking ways to reduce their impact on the planet.

One area where this is particularly important is in woodworking. Wood is a beautiful, natural, and versatile material that has been used for millennia to create everything from furniture to homes. However, the use of wood can also have a significant impact on the environment, particularly when it is not harvested sustainably.

In this chapter, we will explore why woodcraft matters in the 21st century. We will look at the environmental impact of woodworking, the benefits of using sustainable wood, and the role that woodcraft can play in building a more sustainable future. We will also discuss some of the challenges that woodcraft faces in the modern world and how we can overcome them to create a better tomorrow.

Why Woodcraft Matters in the 21st Century

In the 21st century, our society is more aware than ever of the impact we have on the environment. From the food we eat to the products we use, there is a growing recognition that our choices have consequences. As we face the challenges of climate change and biodiversity loss, many people are turning to sustainable practices in an effort to reduce their impact on the planet.

Woodcraft is one area where sustainable practices can have a significant impact. Wood is a beautiful, natural, and versatile material that has been used for thousands of years to create everything from tools to homes. However, the use of wood can also have a significant impact on the environment, particularly when it is not harvested sustainably.

Here are some reasons why woodcraft matters in the 21st century:

- **Environmental Impact:** Woodworking has a significant impact on the environment, particularly when wood is not harvested sustainably. Deforestation, over-harvesting, and illegal logging can lead to habitat destruction, loss of biodiversity, soil erosion, and other environmental problems. By using sustainable wood and practicing responsible woodworking techniques, we can help minimize the environmental impact of woodcraft.

- **Sustainable Materials:** Wood is a renewable resource, which means it can be replenished over time. However, it is important to use wood from sustainable sources that are managed responsibly to ensure the long-term viability of this resource. Sustainable woodcraft can help us meet our needs for wood products while also protecting the environment.

- **Traditional Skills:** Woodworking is an ancient craft that has been practiced for thousands of years. By preserving traditional woodworking skills and techniques, we can honor our cultural heritage and ensure that these skills are passed down to future generations.

- **Beauty and Function:** Wood is a beautiful and versatile material that can be used to create a wide range of functional and aesthetic products. From furniture and home decor to tools and utensils, woodcraft allows us to create useful and beautiful items that enhance our lives.

- **Economic Benefits:** Woodworking can also provide economic benefits for communities and individuals. By using sustainably harvested wood and supporting local woodworking businesses, we can create jobs, stimulate local economies, and promote the use of renewable resources.

Overall, woodcraft matters in the 21st century because it allows us to create beautiful, functional, and sustainable products while also protecting the environment and preserving traditional skills. By embracing sustainable woodcraft, we can build a better future for ourselves and future generations.

The Environmental Impact of Woodworking

Here are some ways that woodworking can impact the environment:

1. **Deforestation:** One of the biggest environmental impacts of woodworking is deforestation. Forests are important ecosystems that support biodiversity, regulate the climate, and provide important resources for human communities. When forests are cleared for timber harvesting, the loss of habitat can lead to the extinction of species and other environmental problems.

2. **Soil Erosion:** Clear-cutting forests can also lead to soil erosion, which can impact water quality, reduce soil fertility, and contribute to flooding and landslides.

3. **Climate Change:** The logging and transportation of wood products can also contribute to climate change by releasing carbon dioxide and other greenhouse gasses into the atmosphere. When forests are cleared, the carbon that was stored in the trees is released, contributing to global warming.

4. **Waste and Pollution:** Woodworking can also generate waste and pollution, particularly when harmful chemicals are used in the finishing process. This can lead to air and water pollution, and can harm human health and wildlife.

5. **Unsustainable Harvesting Practices:** When wood is harvested unsustainably, it can lead to over-harvesting and the depletion of forests. This can have a long-term impact on the environment, including the loss of biodiversity and ecosystem services.

By using sustainable wood and practicing responsible woodworking techniques, we can minimize the environmental impact of woodworking. Sustainable woodcraft can also help protect forests and promote the use of renewable resources.

The Benefits of Using Sustainable Wood

Here are some benefits of using sustainable wood:

1. **Reduced Environmental Impact:** Sustainable wood comes from forests that are managed responsibly, which means that the trees are harvested in a way that protects the forest ecosystem and promotes the long-term health of the forest. This reduces the environmental impact of wood production, including deforestation, soil erosion, and carbon emissions.

2. **Renewable Resource:** Wood is a renewable resource that can be replenished over time. By using sustainable wood, we can ensure that we have a reliable supply of wood products without depleting natural resources.

3. **High-Quality Products:** Sustainable wood is often of a higher quality than wood that is harvested unsustainably. This is because sustainable forestry practices promote healthy forests, which in turn produce stronger and healthier trees.

4. **Economic Benefits:** Sustainable forestry can also provide economic benefits for local communities, including jobs, income, and a source of renewable resources.

5. **Carbon Sequestration:** Trees are natural carbon sinks, which means that they absorb carbon dioxide from the atmosphere and store it in their biomass. By using sustainable wood, we can help to promote the sequestration of carbon and mitigate the impacts of climate change.

Overall, using sustainable wood is a way to promote environmental, economic, and social sustainability. By supporting sustainable forestry practices, we can ensure that we have a reliable supply of wood products without depleting natural resources, while also supporting local communities and protecting the environment.

Woodcraft's Role in Building a more Sustainable Future

Here are some ways that woodcraft can play a role in building a more sustainable future:

- **Sustainable Materials:** Wood is a renewable and sustainable material that can be used in a wide range of products, from furniture to construction materials. By using sustainable wood and other natural materials in woodcraft, we can reduce the environmental impact of our products and promote sustainable practices.

- **Local Sourcing:** Woodcraft can also promote local sourcing of materials, which reduces transportation emissions and supports local economies. By using locally sourced wood, we can reduce the carbon footprint of our products and support sustainable forestry practices in our communities.

- **Longevity:** One of the benefits of woodcraft is that it can produce long-lasting and durable products. By creating high-quality products that are designed to last, we can reduce waste and promote sustainable consumption patterns.

- **Upcycling and Recycling:** Woodcraft can also promote upcycling and recycling, by using reclaimed wood or turning waste wood into new products. This reduces the demand for new wood and reduces the amount of waste that goes to landfills.

- **Education and Awareness:** Finally, woodcraft can play a role in educating people about sustainable practices and raising awareness about environmental issues. By promoting sustainable woodcraft and showcasing the benefits of using sustainable materials, we can encourage people to make more environmentally conscious choices in their everyday lives.

Overall, woodcraft has the potential to play a significant role in building a more sustainable future. By promoting sustainable materials, local sourcing, longevity, upcycling and recycling, and education and awareness, we can create a more sustainable and resilient society.

Future Challenges of Wood Art

Here are some challenges that woodcraft faces in the modern world:

- **Deforestation:** One of the biggest challenges that woodcraft faces is deforestation. As demand for wood products continues to increase, forests are being cleared at an unsustainable rate, which can lead to habitat loss, soil erosion, and other environmental problems.

- **Illegal Logging:** Illegal logging is a major problem in many parts of the world, and can contribute to deforestation, corruption, and social conflict. Illegal logging can also lead to the destruction of protected forests and wildlife habitats, and can harm the livelihoods of local communities who rely on forests for their survival.

- **Sustainability Certification:** While sustainable forestry practices are becoming more common, it can be difficult for consumers to identify sustainable products. Certification schemes like the Forest Stewardship Council (FSC) and the Programme for the Endorsement of Forest Certification (PEFC) can help, but certification can be expensive and time-consuming for small-scale producers.

- **Competition from Synthetic Materials:** Woodcraft also faces competition from synthetic materials like plastic and metal, which can be cheaper and easier to manufacture. While wood is a renewable and sustainable material, it can be more expensive and time-consuming to work with than synthetic materials.

- **Lack of Awareness and Education:** Finally, many people are simply not aware of the environmental impacts of their choices when it comes to wood products. This can make it difficult for sustainable woodcraft producers to compete with cheaper, unsustainably sourced products.

Overall, woodcraft faces a range of challenges in the modern world, from deforestation and illegal logging to competition from synthetic materials and a lack of awareness and education among consumers. However, by promoting sustainable practices and raising awareness about the benefits of using sustainable wood products, we can work to overcome these challenges and build a more sustainable future.

Overcoming Challenges

Here are some ways we can overcome the challenges facing woodcraft to create a better tomorrow:

- **Sustainable Forestry Practices:** One of the most important steps we can take is to promote sustainable forestry practices, which can help to reduce deforestation and promote responsible management of forest resources. Certification schemes like the FSC and PEFC can help to promote sustainable forestry practices and provide consumers with a way to identify sustainable products.

- **Combat Illegal Logging:** We can also work to combat illegal logging by supporting initiatives that promote responsible forest management and cracking down on illegal logging operations. This can involve working with governments, NGOs, and other stakeholders to strengthen regulations and enforcement mechanisms.

- **Promote Sustainable Wood Products:** To promote sustainable woodcraft, we can work to raise awareness about the benefits of using sustainable wood products and provide consumers with more information about the environmental impacts of their choices. This can involve promoting sustainable wood products in retail stores, online marketplaces, and other venues, as well as educating consumers through public outreach campaigns and educational initiatives.

- **Research and Development:** To remain competitive with synthetic materials, we can invest in research and development to improve the efficiency and sustainability of woodcraft production. This can involve developing new technologies and techniques that make it easier and more cost-effective to work with wood, as well as exploring new uses for wood products in areas like construction, transportation, and energy.

- **Collaboration and Partnership:** Finally, we can work to build collaborative partnerships between stakeholders in the woodcraft industry, including producers, retailers, consumers, and policymakers. By working together, we can identify common goals and solutions, share knowledge and expertise, and create a more sustainable and resilient woodcraft industry.

Overall, by promoting sustainable forestry practices, combating illegal logging, promoting sustainable wood products, investing in research and development, and building collaborative partnerships, we can overcome the challenges facing woodcraft and create a better tomorrow for our planet and future generations.

Chapter 2:

The Environmental Impact of Woodworking

"Woodworking is an ancient craft that has been practiced for thousands of years, providing us with everything from furniture and tools to buildings and works of art. However, while wood is a renewable and sustainable resource when managed properly, the environmental impact of woodworking can be significant. In this chapter, we will explore the various ways in which woodworking can affect the environment, including deforestation, habitat destruction, soil erosion, and carbon emissions. We will also look at some of the measures that can be taken to reduce the environmental impact of woodworking, including sustainable forestry practices, responsible sourcing of wood products, and the use of eco-friendly finishes and adhesives. By understanding the environmental impact of woodworking and taking steps to mitigate its effects, we can help to ensure that this ancient craft remains a sustainable and valuable part of our cultural heritage for generations to come."

Can Woodworking Affect the Environment?

Yes, woodworking can affect the environment in a variety of ways. As a primary raw material used in woodworking, wood is often harvested from forests. The demand for wood products can lead to deforestation and habitat destruction, which can have negative impacts on biodiversity and the carbon storage capacity of the forest. In addition, the harvesting of wood can lead to the destruction of wildlife habitats, particularly in old-growth forests. This can disrupt ecosystems, leading to further environmental impacts.

The process of manufacturing wood products can also have environmental impacts. Energy is required to produce and transport wood products, and the waste generated in the production process can contribute to pollution and waste disposal issues. Chemicals used in woodworking products, such as finishes, stains, and adhesives, can be harmful to the environment if not used and disposed of properly.

Woodworking can also contribute to climate change. Deforestation and forest degradation can reduce the carbon storage capacity of forests, releasing carbon dioxide into the atmosphere. The energy used in manufacturing and transportation of wood products can also contribute to greenhouse gas emissions.

However, with the implementation of sustainable forestry practices, responsible sourcing of wood products, and the use of eco-friendly finishes and adhesives, the negative environmental impacts of woodworking can be reduced. By understanding the ways in which woodworking can affect the environment, we can work to promote sustainable woodworking practices that minimize harm to the planet.

Here are some of the ways in which woodworking can affect the environment:

- **Deforestation:** Wood is the primary raw material used in woodworking, and the demand for wood products can lead to deforestation and habitat destruction. When forests are cleared, the biodiversity of the ecosystem is reduced, and the carbon storage capacity of the forest is lost. This can contribute to climate change and have other negative environmental impacts.

- **Habitat Destruction:** In addition to deforestation, the harvesting of wood can lead to the destruction of wildlife habitats, particularly in old-growth forests. This can lead to the loss of biodiversity and disrupt ecosystems, with knock-on effects on the surrounding environment.

- **Soil Erosion:** Clear-cutting forests and other forms of intensive forestry can lead to soil erosion and degradation, particularly in areas with steep slopes or fragile soils. This can lead to nutrient depletion, reduced water quality, and other environmental impacts.

- **Carbon Emissions:** Woodworking can contribute to carbon emissions through a variety of sources, including the energy used in production, transportation, and waste disposal. Additionally, the loss of forest cover and the associated reduction in carbon storage capacity can contribute to climate change.

- **Chemical Pollution:** Many woodworking products, such as finishes, stains, and adhesives, contain chemicals that can be harmful to the environment if not used and disposed of properly. These chemicals can leach into the soil and waterways, polluting the surrounding environment and potentially harming wildlife and human health.

By understanding the various ways in which woodworking can affect the environment, we can work to mitigate these impacts and promote sustainable woodworking practices that minimize harm to the planet.

Measures to reduce the environmental impact of woodworking:

Here are some measures that can be taken to reduce the environmental impact of woodworking:

1. **Sustainable Forestry Practices:** This involves the use of responsible forestry management practices that ensure the long-term health and productivity of forests. This includes sustainable harvesting techniques, reforestation efforts, and protection of biodiversity and wildlife habitats.

2. **Responsible Sourcing of Wood Products:** This involves sourcing wood products from sustainably managed forests, as well as using reclaimed wood and recycled wood products whenever possible. It also involves verifying the

legality of the wood source to prevent the use of illegal or unsustainable wood.

3. **Eco-Friendly Finishes and Adhesives:** This involves the use of low-toxicity finishes, stains, and adhesives that are free from harmful chemicals such as volatile organic compounds (VOCs) and formaldehyde. These eco-friendly products reduce the amount of pollution and harm to the environment during manufacturing, use, and disposal.

4. **Reduce Waste and Recycle:** This involves reducing the amount of wood waste generated during manufacturing by using efficient cutting techniques and reusing scrap wood. It also involves recycling wood products at the end of their life cycle to prevent waste and reduce the need for new wood products.

5. **Energy Efficiency:** This involves implementing energy-efficient practices in manufacturing, such as using renewable energy sources, reducing energy use during production, and using efficient equipment.

By implementing these measures, the negative environmental impacts of woodworking can be reduced, leading to a more sustainable and environmentally friendly industry.

Mitigating the Environmental Impact of Woodworking for a Sustainable Future

Woodworking is an ancient craft that has been valued for centuries, but it also has the potential to cause significant harm to the environment. As we become more aware of the impact of our actions on the planet, it is important to take steps to mitigate the environmental impact of woodworking. By doing so, we can help to ensure that this craft remains a sustainable and valuable part of our cultural heritage for generations to come.

One of the key ways to reduce the environmental impact of woodworking is through sustainable forestry practices. This involves ensuring that the wood used in woodworking comes from responsibly managed forests that are being harvested in a way that does not deplete natural resources or damage ecosystems. By sourcing wood from sustainably managed forests, we can help to protect natural habitats, maintain biodiversity, and ensure the long-term health of the forest.

Another important step in mitigating the environmental impact of woodworking is by reducing waste and recycling. This involves using efficient cutting techniques to reduce the amount of waste generated during production, and reusing or recycling scrap wood whenever possible. By doing so, we can reduce the amount of wood that goes to waste and decrease the need for new wood products, which in turn reduces the impact on forests.

In addition to sustainable forestry and waste reduction, using eco-friendly finishes and adhesives can also help to reduce the environmental impact of woodworking. By using low-toxicity finishes, stains, and adhesives that are free from harmful chemicals, we can reduce pollution and harm to the environment during manufacturing, use, and disposal.

Lastly, energy efficiency is another important aspect of reducing the environmental impact of woodworking. By using renewable energy sources, reducing energy use during production, and using efficient equipment, we can reduce the energy consumption and greenhouse gas emissions associated with woodworking.

In conclusion, mitigating the environmental impact of woodworking is essential for ensuring a sustainable future for this ancient craft. By implementing sustainable forestry practices, reducing waste and recycling, using eco-friendly finishes and adhesives, and increasing energy efficiency, we can help to minimize the negative environmental impacts of woodworking and preserve this valuable cultural heritage for generations to come.

Chapter 3:

Understanding Sustainable Wood Sourcing

In recent years, there has been a growing awareness of the impact that our choices have on the environment, and the importance of sustainable practices in every aspect of our lives. One area where this is particularly relevant is in woodworking, where the sourcing of wood can have a significant impact on the environment. Chapter 3 will explore the importance of responsible wood sourcing in woodworking, and how it can help to create a more sustainable future.

This chapter will delve into the concept of sustainable wood sourcing and what it entails. It will explain the importance of sourcing wood responsibly, including the impact that irresponsible sourcing can have on the environment. This includes deforestation, habitat destruction, and the loss of biodiversity. Additionally, it will outline the role of certifications such as the Forest Stewardship Council (FSC) and the Programme for the Endorsement of Forest Certification (PEFC) in promoting responsible wood sourcing.

The chapter will also cover the various types of wood and their sustainability levels, including the pros and cons of using reclaimed and recycled wood, as well as the importance of selecting wood that is locally sourced to reduce transportation emissions. Furthermore, it will explore the ethical and social considerations associated with wood sourcing, such as fair labor practices and the rights of indigenous communities.

By understanding the importance of responsible wood sourcing, woodworkers can make informed decisions about the materials they use, and contribute to a more sustainable future. This chapter will provide readers with a comprehensive guide to sourcing wood sustainably, including practical tips and advice on how to make environmentally responsible choices when selecting wood for their woodworking projects.

The Importance of Responsible Wood Sourcing in Woodworking

Responsible wood sourcing is crucial in woodworking for several reasons. Firstly, wood is a finite resource, and if not managed sustainably, the demand for wood products can lead to deforestation and habitat destruction, contributing to climate change and the loss of biodiversity. Sustainable wood sourcing ensures that forests are managed responsibly, taking into account ecological, social, and economic factors, and ensuring that forests are preserved for future generations.

Secondly, responsible wood sourcing helps to ensure that the wood used in woodworking is of high quality and free from harmful chemicals. Irresponsible wood sourcing can result in the use of wood that is not fit for purpose, leading to product failure and potentially hazardous working conditions for woodworkers. Moreover, unsustainable forestry practices can lead to the use of pesticides and other harmful chemicals that can pollute water sources and harm wildlife.

Thirdly, responsible wood sourcing can help to support local communities and economies, particularly in rural areas where forestry is a significant source of income. By promoting sustainable forestry practices, responsible wood sourcing can help to ensure that communities have access to long-term employment and income, while also preserving their cultural heritage and traditional ways of life.

Finally, responsible wood sourcing is becoming increasingly important to consumers, who are increasingly concerned about the environmental and ethical impact of the products they buy. By sourcing wood responsibly, woodworkers can meet the growing demand for sustainable products and demonstrate their commitment to sustainability.

In summary, responsible wood sourcing is crucial in woodworking as it helps to ensure that forests are managed sustainably, that wood is of high quality and free from harmful chemicals, and that local communities and economies are supported. By promoting sustainable forestry practices and selecting wood responsibly, woodworkers can help to create a more sustainable and equitable future for all.

Create a more Sustainable Future

Responsible wood sourcing is a critical step towards creating a more sustainable future in several ways. Firstly, by selecting wood from sustainable sources, woodworkers can help to ensure that forests are managed responsibly, preserving these ecosystems for future generations. Sustainable forestry practices can help to reduce deforestation, promote reforestation, and protect biodiversity, all of which are essential for combating climate change and maintaining healthy ecosystems.

Secondly, responsible wood sourcing can help to reduce the environmental impact of woodworking. By using wood that is free from harmful chemicals, woodworkers can help to protect their health and the environment. Furthermore, selecting wood from sustainable sources can help to reduce the carbon footprint of woodworking by promoting local sourcing and reducing the energy required to transport wood products over long distances.

Thirdly, responsible wood sourcing can help to support local communities and economies. By promoting sustainable forestry practices and selecting wood from local sources, woodworkers can help to create long-term employment opportunities and support local businesses. This can help to reduce economic inequality and promote more equitable and sustainable economic development.

Finally, responsible wood sourcing is becoming increasingly important to consumers. By selecting wood from sustainable sources and promoting their commitment to sustainability, woodworkers can meet the growing demand for eco-friendly and socially responsible products. This can help to build customer trust and loyalty while also contributing to a more sustainable and ethical marketplace.

In summary, responsible wood sourcing is essential for creating a more sustainable future. By promoting sustainable forestry practices, reducing the environmental impact of woodworking, supporting local communities and economies, and meeting the growing demand for sustainable products, woodworkers can help to build a more equitable and sustainable world for all.

The Concept of Sustainable Wood Sourcing

Sustainable wood sourcing refers to the practice of responsibly managing forests and selecting wood products that are produced in a manner that preserves the health and biodiversity of the forest, supports local communities, and minimizes environmental impact. This practice involves a range of measures, including:

1. **Certification:** Certification programs, such as the Forest Stewardship Council (FSC) and the Programme for the Endorsement of Forest Certification (PEFC), provide standards and guidelines for responsible forest management. These certifications ensure that wood products come from forests that are managed in a sustainable manner, protecting biodiversity, preventing deforestation, and supporting local communities.

2. **Selective harvesting:** Selective harvesting involves the careful selection of trees for harvesting, leaving behind healthy trees to maintain the health and biodiversity of the forest. This method helps to prevent clear-cutting, which can lead to soil erosion, loss of habitat, and other negative impacts on the environment.

3. **Regeneration:** Sustainable forestry practices involve replanting harvested areas to ensure that the forest continues to regenerate and maintain its ecological functions. This can help to reduce the impact of deforestation and promote reforestation.

4. **Responsible sourcing:** Responsible sourcing involves selecting wood products that are produced in a manner that minimizes environmental impact, such as reducing the use of harmful chemicals, minimizing waste, and promoting sustainable transportation and distribution.

5. **Supporting local communities:** Sustainable forestry practices involve supporting local communities by creating employment opportunities, promoting equitable economic development, and respecting the rights of indigenous peoples and other local communities.

By following these measures, woodworkers can help to ensure that the wood they use comes from sustainable sources and promotes responsible forest management. This can help to reduce the environmental impact of woodworking, preserve forests for future generations, and support sustainable economic development.

The Importance of Sourcing Wood Responsibly

Sourcing wood responsibly is crucial to mitigating the negative impact that irresponsible wood sourcing can have on the environment. Irresponsible wood sourcing can result in deforestation, habitat destruction, loss of biodiversity, and carbon emissions. These issues can contribute to climate change, which has far-reaching consequences for the planet.

Deforestation, which is often the result of irresponsible wood sourcing practices, contributes to climate change by releasing carbon stored in trees into the atmosphere. Forests play a critical role in mitigating climate change by sequestering carbon through photosynthesis. When forests are destroyed, the carbon they store is released into the atmosphere, contributing to greenhouse gas emissions.

Irresponsible wood sourcing can also result in the destruction of habitats for wildlife, leading to a loss of biodiversity. Forests are home to countless species of plants and animals, and their destruction can lead to the extinction of these species. This loss of biodiversity can have cascading effects on the ecosystem, impacting everything from soil health to water quality.

In addition to its impact on the environment, irresponsible wood sourcing can also have negative social and economic impacts. It can lead to the displacement of indigenous communities, as well as the exploitation of workers and local communities. It can also lead to the loss of income for those who rely on the forest for their livelihoods.

In contrast, responsible wood sourcing promotes sustainable forest management, protects biodiversity, and supports local communities. By sourcing wood from certified sustainable sources and supporting responsible forestry practices, woodworkers can help to reduce their impact on the environment, support sustainable economic development, and preserve forests for future generations.

The Importance of Forest Certification in Sustainable Wood Sourcing

Responsible wood sourcing involves promoting sustainable forest management practices that reduce the negative impact of wood production on the environment, as well as on local communities and economies. Forest certification plays a crucial role in promoting responsible wood sourcing and ensuring that wood products are sourced sustainably.

Certification programs such as the Forest Stewardship Council (FSC) and the Programme for the Endorsement of Forest Certification (PEFC) are two of the most widely recognized and respected forest certification systems. These organizations work to promote responsible forest management practices and ensure that wood products are sourced sustainably.

The FSC, for example, sets standards for responsible forest management, including protecting biodiversity, promoting the rights of indigenous peoples, and ensuring that forest workers are treated fairly. Companies that are certified by the FSC must adhere to these standards and are audited regularly to ensure that they continue to meet them.

Similarly, the PEFC works to promote responsible forest management by setting standards for sustainable forestry practices, including protecting wildlife habitats and ensuring that forests are managed in a way that maintains their ecological, social, and economic value.

By choosing to source wood products from certified sources, woodworkers can help to promote responsible forest management practices and ensure that the wood they use is sourced sustainably. This, in turn, can help to mitigate the negative impact of wood production on the environment, protect biodiversity, and support local communities and economies.

In conclusion, forest certification programs like the FSC and PEFC play a critical role in promoting responsible wood sourcing and ensuring that the wood products we use are sourced sustainably. By supporting certified sources and promoting sustainable forest management practices, we can help to create a more sustainable future for ourselves and for generations to come.

Sustainable Wood Choices: Understanding the Pros and Cons of Different Types of Wood

Woodworking is a craft that relies heavily on the use of wood, which can have a significant impact on the environment. Choosing sustainable wood is an essential part of responsible woodworking practices. This chapter will explore the different types of wood and their sustainability levels, including the pros and cons of using reclaimed and recycled wood, as well as the importance of selecting wood that is locally sourced to reduce transportation emissions.

When it comes to sustainable wood choices, there are several factors to consider. One of the most important is the source of the wood. Wood that is sustainably sourced from responsibly managed forests is an excellent choice. It is essential to choose wood from sources that are certified by organizations such as the Forest Stewardship Council (FSC) or the Programme for the Endorsement of Forest Certification (PEFC). These certifications ensure that the wood comes from a well-managed forest and that the wood is harvested in an environmentally responsible manner.

Reclaimed and recycled wood is another excellent choice for sustainable woodworking. Reclaimed wood comes from old buildings, bridges, and other structures that are no longer in use. This wood can be salvaged and repurposed, reducing the demand for new wood and preventing it from ending up in a landfill.

Recycled wood is made from wood scraps and waste that would otherwise be discarded. This wood is processed and used to create new wood products, reducing the need for virgin wood and diverting waste from landfills.

While reclaimed and recycled wood are both sustainable choices, there are some drawbacks to consider. Reclaimed wood can be challenging to work with, as it may be uneven or contain nails and other debris. Recycled wood, on the other hand, may not have the same structural integrity as virgin wood.

Another factor to consider when choosing sustainable wood is transportation emissions. Choosing wood that is locally sourced can help to reduce transportation emissions, as the wood does not have to be transported long distances. This can also help to support local economies and reduce the carbon footprint of the woodworking industry.

In conclusion, there are several factors to consider when choosing sustainable wood for woodworking projects. Sustainable wood choices include wood that is sustainably sourced, reclaimed wood, and recycled wood. While each of these options has its pros and cons, all can help to reduce the impact of woodworking on the environment. Choosing wood that is locally sourced can also help to reduce transportation emissions and support local economies. By making responsible wood choices, woodworkers can help to build a more sustainable future.

Ethical and Social Considerations in Wood Sourcing

Wood sourcing is not only an environmental concern but also an ethical and social issue. The exploitation of workers and disregard for indigenous peoples' rights are some of the challenges associated with wood sourcing.

Environmental standards are not enough to ensure responsible wood sourcing. We need to ensure that the people involved in the process are also treated fairly. In this chapter, we will discuss the ethical and social considerations associated with wood sourcing.

The Impact of Unethical Practices:

Unethical practices in wood sourcing can have severe consequences. For example, in some countries, the exploitation of workers is widespread in the forestry sector. Workers may be subject to poor working conditions, low wages, and exposure to hazardous chemicals.

Moreover, in some cases, the rights of indigenous peoples are ignored, and their ancestral lands are taken away from them. This can have long-lasting effects on their culture and livelihoods.

Fair Labor Practices:

To ensure ethical wood sourcing, it is essential to prioritize fair labor practices. This includes providing workers with safe and healthy working conditions, fair wages, and protecting their rights to form unions and bargain collectively.

Certifications such as the Forest Stewardship Council (FSC) and the Programme for the Endorsement of Forest Certification (PEFC) also have standards for fair labor practices. These certifications ensure that the rights of workers are protected and that they are paid fairly for their work.

Rights of Indigenous Communities:

Indigenous communities have a deep connection to the forests and are often the best stewards of the land. However, their rights are not always respected, and they are often excluded from decision-making processes.

It is crucial to recognize the rights of indigenous communities and involve them in forest management decisions. This can include providing them with legal recognition of their land rights, consulting with them on forest management plans, and sharing the benefits of sustainable forest management.

Wood sourcing is not only an environmental issue but also an ethical and social concern. Ethical and social considerations associated with wood sourcing are crucial to creating a more sustainable future. Fair labor practices, protecting the rights of indigenous communities, and certifications that ensure ethical practices are all vital components of responsible wood sourcing.

48

Section 2: Building a Sustainable Woodshop

Chapter 4: Green Woodworking Tools and Equipment
Chapter 5: Creating an Eco-Friendly Woodworking Space
Chapter 6: Tips for Reducing Waste and Recycling in Your Shop

50

Chapter 4:

Green Woodworking Tools and Equipment

As the world becomes increasingly environmentally conscious, there is a growing demand for sustainable and eco-friendly alternatives to traditional woodworking tools and equipment. In this chapter, we will explore the concept of green woodworking, and the different types of tools and equipment that are available for woodworkers who are looking to reduce their environmental impact. From hand tools to power tools, we will examine the pros and cons of various options, and provide readers with practical advice on how to make the switch to green woodworking.

The Concept of Green Woodworking

Green woodworking is an approach to woodworking that prioritizes sustainability and environmental friendliness. It is a way of working with wood that minimizes the use of non-renewable resources and reduces waste, while also emphasizing the use of traditional hand tools and techniques.

Green woodworking techniques often involve working with freshly cut, or "green," wood rather than seasoned or kiln-dried wood. This can reduce the need for energy-intensive drying processes and can also lead to a more unique and textured finished product. Additionally, green woodworking often involves using locally sourced materials, which can help to reduce transportation emissions and support local economies.

In addition to these techniques, green woodworking also involves using eco-friendly tools and equipment. This can include hand tools made from sustainable materials, such as bamboo or recycled steel, as well as power tools that are designed to be energy-efficient and have low emissions.

Overall, green woodworking is a holistic approach to woodworking that takes into consideration the environmental impact of every aspect of the process, from the sourcing of materials to the final product. By embracing this approach, woodworkers can create beautiful and functional pieces while also doing their part to protect the planet for future generations.

The different types of tools and equipment

Woodworking can be a highly enjoyable and rewarding activity, but it can also have a significant environmental impact, particularly when it comes to the tools and equipment used in the process. However, there are a number of options available for woodworkers who are looking to reduce their carbon footprint and embrace more sustainable practices.

One popular approach to sustainable woodworking is known as "green woodworking". This term refers to a style of woodworking that emphasizes the use of traditional hand tools and techniques, rather than relying on power tools and other modern equipment. By using hand tools, woodworkers can reduce their reliance on electricity, which can help to reduce their carbon footprint.

Another option for green woodworking is to use tools and equipment that are designed with sustainability in mind. For example, some manufacturers produce hand tools made from recycled materials, or using sustainable production processes. Others offer products that are powered by renewable energy sources such as solar power.

In addition to the tools themselves, there are also a number of practices that woodworkers can adopt to reduce their environmental impact. For example, using locally sourced wood can help to reduce transportation emissions, while avoiding exotic or endangered woods can help to protect vulnerable ecosystems. Recycling and properly disposing of sawdust and other waste materials can also help to minimize the environmental impact of woodworking.

Ultimately, by exploring the various options available for green woodworking and making informed choices about the tools and equipment they use, woodworkers can help to minimize their impact on the environment, while still enjoying the many benefits of this timeless craft.

Hand tools

Hand tools are an essential part of a woodworker's toolkit. They are typically operated by hand and do not require electricity or fuel to function, making them an eco-friendly option for woodworking. Hand tools can be categorized into cutting tools, shaping tools, and assembly tools.

Cutting tools include hand saws, chisels, and knives. Hand saws come in various types and sizes, including crosscut saws, rip saws, and dovetail saws. They are used to cut wood along the grain or across the grain. Chisels are used to remove wood and shape it, while knives can be used for delicate carving work.

Shaping tools include rasps, files, and planes. Rasps and files are used to shape wood by removing material, while planes are used to smooth and shape wood by removing thin shavings.

Assembly tools include hammers, mallets, and screwdrivers. These tools are used to put together various pieces of wood, such as joints and fasteners.

In addition to these tools, there are also various hand-powered machines available for woodworking. These include hand-cranked drills, hand-powered lathes, and hand-cranked table saws.

Using hand tools for woodworking has many benefits beyond their eco-friendliness. They require less maintenance, are quieter, and provide a more intimate connection to the wood and the project. Additionally, many woodworkers find that using hand tools enhances their skills and creativity.

List of some Hand Tools:

- Hand saws (e.g. rip saw, crosscut saw, dovetail saw)
- Chisels
- Hand planes (e.g. smoothing plane, jack plane, block plane)
- Hand drills and braces
- Hammers and mallets
- Screwdrivers and hand-held screwdrivers
- Rasp and files
- Handheld sanders and sandpaper
- Handheld routers
- Measuring and marking tools (e.g. tape measures, rulers, marking gauges, square, protractor, compass)

Power tools

Power tools are a staple in modern woodworking, allowing for faster and more precise cuts and shaping than traditional hand tools. However, many power tools can have a significant impact on the environment and contribute to a larger carbon footprint.

There are several steps that woodworkers can take to reduce the environmental impact of their power tools. First, selecting energy-efficient models that consume less power can help to reduce greenhouse gas emissions. Second, choosing tools that are made from sustainable materials can help to reduce the environmental impact of the manufacturing process. Third, proper maintenance and repair of tools can extend their lifespan and reduce the need for replacements.

One emerging trend in green power tools is the use of battery-powered tools. These tools are often more energy-efficient than traditional corded tools and do not require a continuous power source. Additionally, advancements in battery technology have allowed for longer run times and faster charging, making them a viable option for many woodworking applications.

Another trend is the use of recycled and biodegradable materials in tool construction. Companies are increasingly utilizing recycled plastics and metals in their tool designs, as well as using biodegradable lubricants and adhesives to reduce environmental impact.

Overall, it is important for woodworkers to consider the environmental impact of their power tools and choose models that are energy-efficient and made from sustainable materials, as well as properly maintaining and repairing them to extend their lifespan.

List of some Power Tools:

- Circular saws
- Table saws
- Jigsaws
- Band saws
- Compound miter saws
- Radial arm saws
- Planers
- Jointers
- Sanders (e.g. belt sanders, orbital sanders)
- Drills and drill presses
- Routers

- Scroll saws
- Lathe

The pros and cons of various options

Switching to green woodworking tools and equipment requires careful consideration of the pros and cons of various options. While hand tools are generally considered to be more environmentally friendly than power tools, they may not always be the most practical choice. For example, hand saws and planes are ideal for smaller projects, but they may not be efficient for larger projects that require a lot of wood to be cut or shaped.

On the other hand, power tools offer greater speed and precision, making them more efficient for larger projects. However, they typically require electricity to operate, which can increase energy consumption and contribute to carbon emissions. To mitigate this impact, woodworkers can look for energy-efficient power tools or choose models that are powered by renewable energy sources, such as solar or wind power.

Another option for woodworkers looking to reduce their environmental impact is to opt for second-hand tools. This not only reduces waste by giving old tools a new life, but it also avoids the energy-intensive production process associated with new tools. Additionally, choosing tools made from sustainable materials, such as bamboo or recycled plastic, can help to reduce the environmental impact of woodworking.

When making the switch to green woodworking tools and equipment, woodworkers should also consider the maintenance and disposal of their tools. Regular maintenance can extend the lifespan of tools and prevent the need for frequent replacements, while proper disposal ensures that old tools are recycled or disposed of in an environmentally responsible manner.

In summary, choosing green woodworking tools and equipment requires careful consideration of the specific needs of each project, as well as an understanding of the environmental impact of different options. By making informed choices, woodworkers can reduce their environmental footprint and contribute to a more sustainable future.

Chapter 5:

Creating an Eco-Friendly Woodworking Space

Woodworking is a craft that requires not only skill and creativity but also a commitment to sustainability and environmental responsibility. In this chapter, we will delve into the steps woodworkers can take to create an eco-friendly woodworking space. From the layout and organization of the workshop to the materials and finishes used, there are numerous ways to minimize the environmental impact of woodworking practices.

We will explore the principles of eco-friendly woodworking, including reducing waste, conserving energy, and using sustainable materials. We will also delve into the importance of proper ventilation, waste disposal, and the use of non-toxic finishes and adhesives. This chapter will provide readers with practical tips and strategies on how to create a woodworking space that aligns with eco-friendly principles and promotes sustainability in the craft. By implementing these practices, woodworkers can contribute to a greener and more environmentally conscious approach to woodworking, helping to protect our planet for current and future generations. Let's explore the various aspects of creating an eco-friendly woodworking space and the positive impact it can have on the environment.

Creating an Eco-Friendly Woodworking Space

Woodworking is not only about the materials and tools used, but also about the workspace where the magic happens. In this chapter, we will explore the steps woodworkers can take to create an eco-friendly woodworking space. From setting up an efficient layout to managing waste and implementing sustainable practices, creating an environmentally responsible woodworking space can have a significant impact on reducing the environmental footprint of woodworking activities.

We will delve into various aspects of an eco-friendly woodworking space, including:

- **Efficient layout and organization:** Woodworkers can optimize their workspace by designing an efficient layout that minimizes unnecessary movement, reduces material waste, and maximizes the use of natural light. Proper organization of tools, materials, and workstations can enhance productivity while minimizing the environmental impact.

- **Energy-efficient lighting and equipment**: Using energy-efficient lighting, such as LED bulbs, and selecting power tools and equipment with high energy-efficiency ratings can help reduce electricity consumption in the woodworking space. Proper maintenance and usage of tools and equipment can also prolong their lifespan, reducing the need for replacement and waste.

- **Waste management:** Woodworking generates various types of waste, including wood scraps, sawdust, and finishing materials. Implementing proper waste management practices such as recycling, composting, and reusing wood scraps can significantly reduce the environmental impact of woodworking activities.

- **Sustainable material choices:** Woodworkers can make conscious choices when it comes to selecting materials for their woodworking projects. Using sustainably sourced wood, reclaimed wood, or recycled wood can help reduce the demand for new wood and promote responsible wood sourcing practices.

- **Eco-friendly finishes and adhesives:** Choosing eco-friendly finishes and adhesives that are low in volatile organic compounds (VOCs) can minimize indoor air pollution and contribute to a healthier and more eco-friendly woodworking environment.

- **Water conservation:** Woodworking activities may require the use of water for various purposes, such as cleaning tools and finishes. Implementing water-saving practices, such as using water-efficient equipment and collecting and reusing rainwater, can help reduce water consumption in the woodworking space.

By implementing these and other sustainable practices, woodworkers can create an eco-friendly woodworking space that is not only environmentally responsible but also conducive to productivity and creativity. Taking steps to minimize the environmental impact of woodworking activities in the workspace can contribute to a greener future for the woodworking community and the planet as a whole. In the following chapters, we will delve deeper into each of these aspects and provide practical tips and guidance for woodworkers to create an eco-friendly woodworking space. Stay tuned for valuable insights on how to make your woodworking space more sustainable!

Practical Tips for Reducing Environmental Impact

!Here are some practical tips for woodworkers to reduce their environmental impact in their woodworking practices:

1. **Use sustainable and responsibly sourced wood**: Choose wood that is certified by organizations such as the Forest Stewardship Council (FSC) or the Programme for the Endorsement of Forest Certification (PEFC) to ensure it is harvested using environmentally responsible practices.

2. **Opt for reclaimed or recycled wood:** Consider using reclaimed or recycled wood, which reduces the demand for newly harvested wood and minimizes waste. This can include salvaging

wood from old furniture, buildings, or other sources.

3. **Select local wood:** Choose wood that is locally sourced to reduce the carbon footprint associated with transportation emissions. Locally sourced wood can also support local economies and reduce the environmental impact of long-distance shipping.

4. **Minimize waste:** Practice efficient woodworking techniques to minimize waste. Plan your projects carefully to maximize the use of wood and minimize scrap. Consider repurposing or recycling wood scraps rather than discarding them.

5. **Use eco-friendly finishes and adhesives:** Opt for eco-friendly finishes and adhesives that have lower VOC (Volatile Organic Compounds) content and are safer for the environment and human health. Look for water-based or plant-based finishes, adhesives, and glues as alternatives to traditional solvent-based options.

6. **Conserve energy:** Implement energy-saving practices in your woodworking workshop, such as using energy-efficient lighting, turning off tools and equipment when not in use, and insulating your workshop to reduce heating or cooling needs.

7. **Properly dispose of waste:** Follow proper waste disposal practices, including recycling,

composting, and hazardous waste disposal, to minimize the environmental impact of waste generated from woodworking activities.

8. **Consider alternative materials**: Explore alternative materials to wood, such as bamboo, cork, or reclaimed materials, which may have a lower environmental impact and may be more sustainable for certain woodworking applications.

9. **Educate yourself:** Stay informed about best practices for environmentally responsible woodworking by keeping up-to-date with relevant certifications, regulations, and guidelines for sustainable woodworking practices.

By incorporating these practical tips into their woodworking practices, woodworkers can reduce their environmental impact and contribute to a more sustainable approach to woodworking, helping to protect the environment and create a better future for generations to come. Remember, small changes in our woodworking practices can collectively make a significant positive impact on the environment. Happy and eco-friendly woodworking!

The principles of eco-friendly woodworking

Woodworking, like any other craft or industry, has an impact on the environment. From the sourcing of materials to the use of tools and finishes, woodworkers have the opportunity to make conscious choices that can significantly reduce their environmental footprint. In this chapter, we will explore the principles of eco-friendly woodworking, focusing on practical tips for reducing environmental impact.

1. **Reduce Waste:** One of the key principles of eco-friendly woodworking is minimizing waste. This can be achieved by carefully planning projects to minimize excess material, reusing or repurposing wood scraps, and properly disposing of wood waste. Woodworkers can also consider using reclaimed or recycled wood, salvaging wood from old furniture or buildings, and incorporating wood with natural defects or character into their projects.

2. **Conserve Energy:** Woodworking often involves the use of power tools, which can consume a significant amount of energy. Woodworkers can reduce their energy consumption by investing in energy-efficient tools, using tools with variable speed settings, and turning off tools when not in use. Additionally, using hand tools or foot-powered tools, such as a foot-powered lathe, can help reduce energy consumption.

3. **Use Sustainable Materials:** The choice of materials used in woodworking can have a significant impact on the environment. Woodworkers can opt for sustainably harvested wood that is certified by organizations like the Forest Stewardship Council (FSC) or the Programme for the Endorsement of Forest

Certification (PEFC). They can also consider using alternative materials, such as bamboo or reclaimed wood, which are known for their sustainable properties. Additionally, using water-based or low-VOC (volatile organic compounds) finishes and adhesives can reduce harmful emissions and minimize the impact on indoor air quality.

4. **Practice Responsible Wood Sourcing:** Woodworkers can make a positive impact on the environment by sourcing wood responsibly. This includes choosing wood from responsibly managed forests, supporting local wood suppliers to reduce transportation emissions, and avoiding wood from endangered or protected species. Woodworkers can also prioritize fair labor practices, ensuring that the wood they use is harvested and processed ethically, and that the rights of indigenous communities are respected.

5. **Practice Efficient Workshop Organization:** Organizing the woodworking workshop efficiently can also contribute to eco-friendly woodworking practices. This includes proper storage and handling of materials to prevent waste and damage, implementing effective dust collection systems to minimize air pollution, and using energy-efficient lighting in the workshop. Properly maintaining tools and equipment can also extend their lifespan, reducing the need for frequent replacements and ultimately reducing waste.

By implementing these principles and tips, woodworkers can make a significant difference in reducing their environmental impact and promoting eco-friendly woodworking practices. Being mindful of the materials, tools, finishes, and practices used in woodworking can lead to a more sustainable and responsible approach to this craft, contributing to a better future for our planet.

Note: It's always important to research and stay updated on best practices for eco-friendly woodworking, as materials, technologies, and regulations may change over time. Consulting with local environmental regulations and guidelines is also recommended to ensure compliance with regional laws and regulations. So, woodworkers should always stay informed and continuously strive to improve their eco-friendly woodworking practices.

Creating an Eco-Friendly Woodworking Space Impact

Woodworkers can take several steps to create an eco-friendly woodworking space that minimizes their environmental impact. These steps include not only the layout and organization of the workshop, but also considerations such as waste disposal, ventilation, and the use of non-toxic finishes and adhesives.

1. **Proper ventilation**: Good ventilation is crucial in a woodworking space to ensure that dust and fumes are properly filtered and not released into the air. Woodworkers should invest in high-quality dust collection systems and exhaust fans

to effectively capture and filter airborne particles. This helps to create a healthier and safer working environment for woodworkers and reduces the impact of dust and fumes on the surrounding environment.

2. **Waste disposal:** Proper waste disposal is essential in an eco-friendly woodworking space. Woodworkers should implement a waste management system that includes sorting and recycling of wood scraps, sawdust, and other waste materials. Wood scraps can be repurposed for other projects or donated to local woodworkers or schools for creative use. Sawdust can be used for composting or as a natural mulch in the garden. By minimizing waste and implementing responsible waste disposal practices, woodworkers can reduce their environmental impact.

3. **Non-toxic finishes and adhesives**: Traditional finishes and adhesives used in woodworking often contain harmful chemicals that can be detrimental to human health and the environment. Woodworkers should opt for non-toxic finishes and adhesives that are water-based, low-VOC (Volatile Organic Compounds), and environmentally friendly. There are many eco-friendly finishes and adhesives available on the market that are made from natural ingredients and are biodegradable. Using these types of finishes and adhesives helps to reduce the release of harmful chemicals into the

environment and promotes a healthier living and working environment.

4. **Conservation of energy:** Woodworking often requires the use of power tools, which can consume significant amounts of energy. Woodworkers can reduce their environmental impact by using energy-efficient tools and equipment, as well as implementing energy-saving practices in their woodworking space. This may include using LED lighting, turning off tools and equipment when not in use, and optimizing the use of natural light. Additionally, woodworkers can consider investing in renewable energy sources such as solar panels to power their workshop, further reducing their reliance on fossil fuels and minimizing their carbon footprint.

5. **Use of sustainable materials:** Choosing sustainable materials for woodworking projects is another important aspect of eco-friendly woodworking. Woodworkers should opt for wood that is certified by reputable organizations such as the Forest Stewardship Council (FSC) or the Programme for the Endorsement of Forest Certification (PEFC), which ensures that the wood is harvested from sustainably managed forests. Woodworkers can also consider using reclaimed or recycled wood, which reduces the demand for new wood and helps to conserve natural resources. Additionally, using locally sourced wood helps to reduce transportation

emissions associated with long-distance wood transport.

By implementing these practical tips and principles of eco-friendly woodworking, woodworkers can significantly reduce their environmental impact and contribute to a more sustainable woodworking practice. Taking steps to properly manage waste, promote good ventilation, use non-toxic finishes and adhesives, conserve energy, and choose sustainable materials can all contribute to creating an eco-friendly woodworking space that is environmentally responsible and beneficial for both woodworkers and the environment. So, it's important for woodworkers to be mindful of their practices and strive to reduce their environmental footprint in their woodworking activities.

Note: It's always recommended for woodworkers to follow local regulations and guidelines related to waste disposal, ventilation, and the use of finishes and adhesives, and to choose materials that are locally available and comply with relevant sustainability certifications in their region. Regulations and practices may vary

Chapter 6: Tips for Reducing Waste and Recycling in Your Shop

Woodworking can generate a significant amount of waste, which can have a negative impact on the environment if not managed properly. From sawdust and scraps to packaging and shipping materials, waste is an inevitable byproduct of woodworking. However, there are various ways in which woodworkers can reduce waste and recycle materials in their shops, ultimately creating a more sustainable and eco-friendly woodworking practice.

Reducing waste is important not only for the environment but also for cost savings and efficient use of resources. Proper waste management can also help minimize the amount of waste that ends up in landfills or polluting our natural ecosystems. In this chapter, we will explore the various ways in which woodworkers can reduce waste and recycle materials in their shops.

We will discuss the importance of reducing waste, the environmental impact of waste disposal, and practical tips for recycling materials such as sawdust, scrap wood, and shipping materials. Additionally, we will cover the benefits of upcycling and repurposing materials, as well as the role of composting in reducing waste in the woodworking industry. By adopting these practices, woodworkers can help create a more sustainable future and minimize their impact on the environment.

The Various Ways in which Woodworkers Can Reduce Waste

here are some practical ways to reduce waste in a woodworking shop:

Plan your projects carefully: One of the biggest contributors to waste in woodworking is over-cutting or mis-measuring materials. By taking the time to plan your projects carefully, you can minimize the amount of excess material that is generated.

Use scraps creatively: Rather than throwing away scraps of wood, try to find creative ways to use them in future projects. For example, small pieces of wood can be used to make decorative accents or trim pieces.

Donate or sell usable materials: If you have leftover materials that you don't plan on using, consider donating or selling them to other woodworkers. This can help to reduce waste and prevent usable materials from ending up in landfills.

Invest in a dust collection system: Sawdust is a common byproduct of woodworking, but it can be harmful to both the environment and your health if not properly disposed of. A dust collection system can help to capture sawdust and other debris, making it easier to dispose of in an environmentally responsible way.

Use eco-friendly finishes: Many traditional wood finishes contain harsh chemicals that can be harmful to the environment. Look for eco-friendly finishes that are made with natural, non-toxic ingredients instead.

Choose sustainable materials: Using sustainable materials such as FSC-certified wood or reclaimed wood can help to reduce the amount of waste generated in the woodworking process. Additionally, using sustainable materials can help to support responsible forestry practices and protect natural resources.

The Importance of Reducing Waste

Reducing waste is crucial for creating a sustainable future. Waste can have a significant environmental impact, contributing to landfills and polluting the air, water, and soil. The production of waste also requires resources, such as energy and materials, which can be conserved by reducing waste. In addition, reducing waste can lead to cost savings for individuals and businesses.

In the woodworking industry, reducing waste can have a significant impact on the environment. Wood waste, in particular, can contribute to greenhouse gas emissions and deforestation if not properly disposed of or recycled. By reducing wood waste, woodworkers can help to conserve resources, reduce pollution, and promote sustainability.

There are various ways in which woodworkers can reduce waste, including using efficient designs and production methods, sourcing materials sustainably, and implementing recycling and waste management systems. By taking steps to reduce waste, woodworkers can create a more eco-friendly woodworking practice and contribute to a more sustainable future.

Reducing waste is crucial for protecting the environment and conserving resources. The production and disposal of waste can have a significant impact on the environment, including air and water pollution, greenhouse gas emissions, and the depletion of natural resources. In addition, waste disposal can also have negative impacts on human health and well-being, particularly for those living in close proximity to landfills and incinerators.

When it comes to woodworking, waste reduction is particularly important due to the large quantities of wood scraps and sawdust generated during the production process. Proper waste disposal can also be costly for woodworkers, particularly for those who need to pay for disposal or recycling services.

By implementing waste reduction strategies, woodworkers can minimize their environmental impact and save money on waste disposal. These strategies can include reducing the amount of waste generated through careful planning and material selection, reusing or repurposing waste materials, and recycling materials whenever possible.

In addition to reducing the environmental impact of waste disposal, these strategies can also have economic benefits for woodworkers, such as reducing material costs and improving efficiency in the production process. Overall, reducing waste is a crucial component of eco-friendly woodworking and can help woodworkers create a more sustainable practice.

Practical Tips for Recycling Materials

The benefits and challenges of upcycling and repurposing materials in woodworking projects.

One practical tip for recycling sawdust is to use it as a mulch for plants or as a filler for compost. Sawdust can also be used as a non-toxic absorbent material for spills in the workshop or as a source of heat for wood stoves.

Scrap wood can be repurposed for smaller projects or used as kindling for fires. Larger pieces of scrap wood can be cut into smaller pieces for use as shims or supports.

Shipping materials such as cardboard boxes and bubble wrap can be reused for shipping materials to customers or for storage and organization in the workshop.

Upcycling and repurposing materials can also be a sustainable option for woodworking projects. Old furniture, doors, and even pallets can be disassembled and repurposed for new projects. While this can require more effort in terms of preparation and cleaning of the materials, it can also result in unique and interesting pieces.

Overall, reducing waste and recycling materials in the woodworking shop can not only have a positive impact on the environment but can also lead to cost savings and creative solutions for projects. proper disposal of hazardous materials such as paint and chemicals is also important to consider.

- **Sawdust and Wood Shavings:** Sawdust and wood shavings can be used for various purposes in the workshop. They can be used as a natural absorbent for spills, as kindling for fires, or as mulch for plants. Woodworkers can also consider donating sawdust and shavings to local farms or animal sanctuaries for use as animal bedding.

- **Scrap Wood:** Instead of throwing away scrap wood, woodworkers can repurpose it for other projects or use it as kindling for fires. Scrap wood can also be donated to community organizations such as schools, community centers, or non-profit organizations for use in art and craft projects.

- **Shipping Materials:** When receiving packages with packing materials, woodworkers can reuse them in their own shipments or donate them to local shipping stores or community organizations. This can help reduce the amount of plastic packaging materials that end up in landfills.

- **Proper Disposal of Hazardous Materials:** Woodworkers should always be mindful of the hazardous materials they use in their workshop such as chemicals and paints. It is important to properly dispose of these materials by taking them to a designated hazardous waste disposal facility. Some local communities also offer hazardous waste pickup services for residents.

By implementing these practical tips, woodworkers can reduce their waste and minimize their impact on the environment.

The Benefits of Upcycling and Repurposing Materials

Upcycling and repurposing materials in woodworking can have significant environmental benefits. When woodworkers upcycle or repurpose materials, they divert waste from landfills, reduce the need for new materials, and conserve natural resources. For example, using reclaimed or salvaged wood for a project can prevent new trees from being cut down, while repurposing an old wooden pallet can reduce the need for new lumber.

Composting is another way to reduce waste in woodworking. By composting sawdust and other organic materials, woodworkers can create a nutrient-rich soil amendment that can be used in gardens or landscaping. Composting also helps to reduce greenhouse gas emissions, as organic waste in landfills contributes to the release of methane, a potent greenhouse gas.

In addition to reducing waste, upcycling, repurposing, and composting can also be cost-effective for woodworkers. Using reclaimed materials or repurposing old items can often be cheaper than buying new materials. Composting can also help to reduce the cost of waste disposal.

Overall, incorporating these practices into woodworking can help to create a more sustainable future and minimize the environmental impact of the industry. By reducing waste and conserving resources, woodworkers can help to protect natural ecosystems and promote a healthier planet for future generations.

Section 3: Eco-Friendly Woodworking Techniques

- Chapter 7: Understanding Wood Joinery and Adhesives
- Chapter 8: Finishing Wood with Natural Products
- Chapter 9: Working with Salvaged and Reclaimed Wood

Chapter 7: Understanding Wood Joinery and Adhesives

Woodworking is an ancient craft that has been practiced for centuries. One of the most important aspects of woodworking is joinery, which refers to the methods used to connect two or more pieces of wood together. Joinery techniques range from simple butt joints to complex mortise and tenon joints, and the choice of joinery method can greatly affect the strength, durability, and appearance of a woodworking project.

In addition to joinery, another important aspect of woodworking is the use of adhesives to bond pieces of wood together. While traditional joinery methods rely on the mechanical strength of the joint, adhesives can provide additional strength and durability to a woodworking project.

This chapter will explore the various techniques and methods used in wood joinery and adhesive applications, including their strengths and weaknesses, as well as tips for selecting the right method for your project. Understanding these techniques is essential for any woodworker looking to create high-quality, long-lasting projects with minimal environmental impact.

Introduction to wood joinery and adhesives

Wood joinery and adhesives are two essential components of woodworking that play a critical role in the strength and durability of a project. Joinery refers to the methods used to connect two pieces of wood together, while adhesives are used to bond pieces of wood together.

Here are some important points to consider when exploring wood joinery and adhesives:

Joinery methods can vary depending on the application and desired look of the project. Some common types of joinery include butt joints, lap joints, mortise and tenon joints, dovetail joints, and finger joints.

The type of joinery used can affect the strength and durability of a project. For example, dovetail joints are known for their strength and are commonly used in furniture construction, while butt joints are less strong and may be used in less demanding applications.

Adhesives can be used in conjunction with joinery to provide additional strength and stability to a project. Common types of adhesives include PVA glue, epoxy, and polyurethane glue.

Different types of adhesives have different strengths and weaknesses. For example, PVA glue is easy to work with and dries clear, but is not as strong as epoxy. Epoxy, on the other hand, is very strong but can be difficult to work with and may require special safety precautions.

The choice of adhesive will depend on the specific application and requirements of the project. Some factors to consider when choosing an adhesive include strength, drying time, and compatibility with the type of wood being used.

Overall, understanding wood joinery and adhesives is critical for creating strong and durable woodworking projects. The proper selection and application of these techniques can help ensure the longevity and quality of a project for years to come.

Traditional wood joinery techniques:

Traditional wood joinery techniques are an important aspect of woodworking, as they offer a strong and durable way to join pieces of wood together. These techniques have been used for centuries and continue to be popular today due to their aesthetic appeal and reliable performance.

One of the most common traditional wood joinery techniques is the mortise and tenon joint. This involves cutting a square or rectangular hole (the mortise) into one piece of wood, and then creating a matching protruding piece (the tenon) on the end of the other piece of wood that fits snugly into the mortise. Mortise and tenon joints are extremely strong and are often used in furniture construction.

Another popular traditional wood joinery technique is the dovetail joint. This joint is typically used to join two pieces of wood at right angles, and consists of interlocking fan-shaped notches cut into each piece of wood. Dovetail joints are known for their strength and resistance to being pulled apart, and are often used in drawer construction.

Finger joints are also a traditional wood joinery technique, and involve interlocking small, rectangular notches cut into the ends of two pieces of wood. Finger joints are typically used for joining pieces of wood that are the same thickness, and are often used in box and drawer construction.

Overall, traditional wood joinery techniques offer a wide range of options for creating strong and durable joints in woodworking projects. By understanding the strengths and weaknesses of each technique, woodworkers can choose the appropriate method for their specific project needs.

Modern wood joinery techniques:

Modern wood joinery techniques have become increasingly popular in recent years due to their efficiency and ease of use. In this section, we will explore some of the most commonly used modern wood joinery techniques, their strengths and weaknesses, and when they are appropriate to use.

- **Biscuit Joinery:** Biscuit joinery involves cutting a small, oval-shaped hole into two pieces of wood and inserting a wooden biscuit (a thin, oval-shaped piece of wood) coated in glue into each hole. The two pieces are then clamped together until the glue dries. This technique is fast, easy, and effective for aligning two pieces of wood, but it may not provide the same strength as traditional joinery techniques.

- **Pocket-hole Joinery**: Pocket-hole joinery involves drilling a hole at an angle into one piece of wood and joining it to another piece of wood with a special screw that is designed to pull the two pieces together. This technique is quick and easy, and the screws can be hidden, but it may not provide the same strength as traditional joinery techniques.

- **Dowel Joinery:** Dowel joinery involves drilling a hole into two pieces of wood and inserting a wooden dowel coated in glue into each hole. The two pieces are then clamped together until the glue dries. This technique is strong and easy to use, but it can be time-consuming and may not provide the same precision as other modern joinery techniques.

Each modern joinery technique has its strengths and weaknesses, and choosing the appropriate technique depends on the project at hand. Biscuit joinery is great for aligning two pieces of wood quickly, while pocket-hole joinery is ideal for hidden screws. Dowel joinery is a strong and reliable technique, but it may take more time and precision to execute properly. By understanding the strengths and weaknesses of each technique, woodworkers can make informed decisions about which technique to use for their specific project.

Types of wood adhesives:

Wood adhesives play a crucial role in the woodworking industry as they help in creating strong and durable joints. There are different types of wood adhesives available, each with its unique properties and advantages. Here are some of the most common types of wood adhesives:

- **PVA (Polyvinyl Acetate) Adhesive:** PVA adhesive is a water-based glue that is widely used in woodworking projects. It dries quickly, is easy to use, and creates a strong bond. PVA adhesive is ideal for indoor projects and is suitable for bonding porous materials like wood, paper, and fabric.

- **Epoxy Adhesive:** Epoxy is a two-part adhesive that consists of a resin and a hardener. It creates a strong and waterproof bond and is ideal for bonding materials that are difficult to join, such as metal and plastic. Epoxy adhesive is also heat-resistant and can withstand exposure to chemicals.

- **Cyanoacrylate Adhesive:** Also known as super glue, cyanoacrylate adhesive is a fast-drying adhesive that creates a strong bond. It is ideal for small projects and for bonding materials that have a tight fit.

- **Polyurethane Adhesive:** Polyurethane adhesive is a two-part adhesive that creates a strong and waterproof bond. It is ideal for outdoor projects and for bonding materials that are difficult to join, such as metal and plastic. Polyurethane adhesive is also heat-resistant and can withstand exposure to chemicals.

When selecting a wood adhesive, it is important to consider the properties of the materials being bonded and the conditions under which the project will be used. Each type of adhesive has its own strengths and weaknesses and is suitable for different applications. For example, PVA adhesive is ideal for indoor projects while polyurethane adhesive is better suited for outdoor projects. Understanding the properties and applications of different types of adhesives can help woodworkers select the right adhesive for their project, ensuring a strong and durable bond.

Strength and durability of wood joints:

The strength and durability of wood joints is a critical aspect of woodworking. The overall quality of a woodworking project depends on the strength and integrity of the joints used to assemble it. Here are some factors that can affect the strength and durability of wood joints:

- **Wood species:** Different wood species have different physical properties, such as density and hardness, which can affect the strength of a joint. Some woods are stronger than others and can better resist shear and tension forces.

- **Grain orientation:** The orientation of the wood grain in a joint can greatly impact its strength. For example, a joint with end-grain to end-grain contact is weaker than a joint with long-grain to long-grain contact.

- **Adhesive type:** The type of adhesive used in a joint can significantly affect its strength and durability. Some adhesives have better resistance to moisture, temperature changes, and impact than others.

- **Joint design:** The design of a joint also plays a crucial role in its strength and durability. A well-designed joint can distribute stress evenly and avoid concentration of stress points, which can lead to failure.

It is essential to consider all these factors when choosing the appropriate joint and adhesive for a specific woodworking project. By selecting the right combination of wood species, grain orientation, adhesive type, and joint design, woodworkers can create strong and durable joints that will last for years.

Importance of proper application:

Proper application of wood adhesives and joinery techniques is critical to ensure the strength, durability, and overall quality of a woodworking project. The following are some important factors to consider for proper application:

- **Surface preparation:** Before applying any adhesive or joining technique, it is important to properly prepare the surfaces to be joined. This may involve cleaning the surfaces, removing any dirt or debris, and sanding or planing to ensure a flat and smooth surface.

- **Clamping:** Proper clamping is essential to ensure a strong and secure joint. The amount and type of clamping pressure required will depend on the type of adhesive and joint being used, as well as the size and shape of the project.

- **Curing time:** All wood adhesives require a certain amount of curing time to reach their full strength. It is important to follow the manufacturer's recommended curing time and avoid moving or stressing the joint too soon.

- **Temperature and humidity:** The temperature and humidity of the workshop can also impact the effectiveness of wood adhesives and joinery techniques. It is important to follow the manufacturer's recommended temperature and humidity ranges for optimal results.

By taking these factors into consideration and following proper application techniques, woodworkers can ensure the strength and durability of their projects, as well as reduce the risk of joint failure over time.

Sustainability considerations:

Here are some points that can be explored in the section on sustainability considerations:

Environmental impact of traditional and modern joinery techniques:

Traditional joinery techniques typically require more skill and time but result in stronger joints with no need for additional hardware or materials. Modern joinery techniques, on the other hand, may be quicker and easier to execute but often require additional hardware or materials like biscuits, dowels, or pocket screws. This can result in more waste and a larger carbon footprint.

Choosing sustainable wood adhesives:

Woodworkers can choose adhesives that are free of harmful chemicals and solvents, as well as those made from sustainable sources. For example, some PVA adhesives are made from plant-based materials and have low VOC (volatile organic compound) emissions.

Reducing waste in joinery and adhesive application:

Proper application of joinery techniques and adhesives can minimize waste and reduce the need for additional materials. For example, using the right amount of adhesive and clamping pressure can reduce squeeze-out and excess adhesive, while careful layout and cutting can minimize scrap wood in joinery applications.

Choosing sustainably sourced wood:

In addition to choosing sustainable adhesives, woodworkers can also make a difference by selecting wood from responsibly managed forests or from salvaged sources. This can help reduce the impact of deforestation and promote sustainable forestry practices.

Consideration of product end-of-life:

Woodworkers can also consider the end-of-life of their products and choose joinery and adhesive techniques that allow for easy disassembly and recycling or reuse of materials. This can help reduce waste and promote a circular economy approach to woodworking.

Tips and tricks for successful joinery and adhesive application:

Here are some tips and tricks for successful joinery and adhesive application in woodworking:

1. **Practice proper surface preparation**: Ensure that the surfaces to be joined are clean, dry, and free from any debris or dust that may interfere with the adhesive's bonding ability.

2. **Use the right adhesive:** Choose an adhesive that is appropriate for the specific project, taking into consideration factors such as the type of wood being used, the level of strength required, and any environmental concerns.

3. **Achieve tight-fitting joints**: Take the time to measure and cut the joint pieces accurately to achieve a tight fit. If the joint is not tight, the adhesive may not be able to create a strong bond.

4. **Use alternative clamping methods:** Consider using alternative clamping methods such as spring clamps, tape, or rubber bands if traditional clamps cannot be used in certain areas of the project.

5. **Avoid glue drips:** Use a minimal amount of adhesive to avoid excess glue drips. Any excess glue can be cleaned up with a damp cloth or sponge.

6. **Allow sufficient curing time:** Follow the adhesive manufacturer's instructions regarding curing time. Rushing the curing process may result in a weaker bond.

7. **Test joints and adhesive strength:** Test the strength of joints and adhesives before proceeding with the final assembly. This can help identify any weak points that need to be addressed before the final assembly.

By following these tips and tricks, woodworkers can achieve strong and durable joints and adhesive applications in their projects.

The Various Techniques and Methods

Here are some techniques and methods used in wood joinery and adhesive applications, including their strengths and weaknesses:

Traditional Joinery Techniques:

Traditional joinery techniques have been used for centuries to create strong and durable wooden structures. Some of the most common traditional joinery techniques include mortise and tenon joints, dovetail joints, and box joints.

Mechanical Joinery Techniques:

Mechanical joinery techniques involve the use of specialized tools to create joints quickly and accurately. These techniques are often used in mass production woodworking. Some examples of mechanical joinery techniques include biscuit joints, dowel joints, and pocket hole joinery.

Adhesive Applications:

Adhesives are used to bond pieces of wood together. There are several types of adhesives available, including PVA (polyvinyl acetate) glue, epoxy, and cyanoacrylate glue. Each type of adhesive has its own strengths and weaknesses.

Strengths of Wood Joinery:

- Traditional joinery techniques are known for their strength and durability.
- Mechanical joinery techniques are often quicker and easier to execute, making them ideal for large-scale production.
- Weaknesses of Wood Joinery:

- Traditional joinery techniques can be time-consuming and require a high level of skill to execute correctly.
- Mechanical joinery techniques may not be as strong as traditional joinery techniques and can sometimes fail under heavy loads.
- Strengths of Adhesive Applications:
- Adhesives can create strong bonds between pieces of wood, even when the joint is not visible.
- Adhesives are often quick and easy to apply, making them ideal for small woodworking projects.

Weaknesses of Adhesive Applications:

- Adhesives may not be as strong as traditional or mechanical joinery techniques.
- Adhesives may require special equipment or tools for application and may not be suitable for all types of wood.

Understanding the various techniques and methods used in wood joinery and adhesive applications is important for woodworkers to create strong and durable wooden structures. By knowing the strengths and weaknesses of each technique, woodworkers can choose the best method for their specific woodworking project.

Chapter 8: Finishing Wood with Natural Products

Wood finishing is an essential part of any woodworking project, as it not only enhances the aesthetic appeal but also protects the wood from wear and tear. In recent years, there has been a growing interest in using natural products for wood finishing, as they are often more eco-friendly and safer to use than traditional chemical-based finishes. In this chapter, we will explore the various techniques and methods of finishing wood with natural products, including their benefits and drawbacks. We will also discuss the best practices for achieving a smooth and durable finish that not only looks great but also helps to preserve the natural beauty of the wood.

The Various Techniques and Methods of Finishing Wood

Woodworkers have been using natural products for centuries to finish and protect their creations. In recent years, there has been a renewed interest in using natural products to achieve a more eco-friendly and sustainable approach to woodworking.

Here is an exploration of the various techniques and methods of finishing wood with natural products:

1. **Oils**: Oils are a popular choice for finishing wood as they penetrate deeply into the wood fibers and provide a natural look and feel. Some

common oils used in woodworking include linseed oil, tung oil, and Danish oil. These oils can enhance the color and grain of the wood, as well as protect it from moisture and scratches. However, oils may require multiple coats and have a longer drying time than other finishing options.

2. **Waxes:** Waxes are another natural finishing option that can provide a soft, matte finish to wood. Beeswax, carnauba wax, and paraffin wax are commonly used in woodworking. Waxes can provide a protective layer on top of the wood and help to repel water and stains. However, they may not be as durable as other finishes and may require reapplication over time.

3. **Shellacs:** Shellac is a natural resin that can be used as a wood finish. It can provide a glossy or matte finish and is often used as a sealer before applying other finishes. Shellac is easy to apply and dries quickly, but may not be as durable as other finishes and can be damaged by alcohol and heat.

4. **Milk Paint:** Milk paint is a natural and environmentally friendly option for finishing wood. It is made from a combination of milk protein, lime, and pigment and can provide a matte or slightly glossy finish. Milk paint is easy to apply and can be sanded and distressed to create a vintage look. However, it may require multiple coats and has a longer drying time than other finishes.

When selecting a natural product for finishing wood, it is important to consider the specific requirements of the project and the desired look and feel of the finished product. Additionally, it is important to follow the manufacturer's instructions for application and to ensure proper ventilation when working with natural finishes.

Benefits and Drawbacks

Here are some benefits and drawbacks of each of the natural products commonly used for finishing wood:

Oils (such as linseed, tung, and walnut oils)
- Benefits: Enhance the natural beauty of the wood, penetrate deeply into the wood fibers for a long-lasting finish, provide some degree of water resistance, and can be easily reapplied when needed.
- Drawbacks: Can take a long time to dry, may require multiple coats for adequate protection, can darken or yellow over time, and can be flammable during application.

Waxes (such as beeswax and carnauba wax)
- Benefits: Provide a natural-looking finish that enhances the wood grain, create a protective layer against moisture and dirt, can be easily buffed to a shine, and are easy to repair or renew.
- Drawbacks: Can require frequent reapplication, can be difficult to remove, may not provide enough protection against scratches or heavy use, and may require solvents for application.

Shellacs (such as dewaxed shellac and seedlac)
- Benefits: Provide a beautiful, clear finish that enhances the wood grain, dry quickly, are easy to apply, and can be easily repaired or touched up.
- Drawbacks: May not provide enough protection against water or scratches, can be susceptible to heat and alcohol damage, and may not be suitable for outdoor use.

Milk paint (made from milk protein, lime, and pigments)
- Benefits: Create a unique, rustic look that enhances the natural texture and grain of the wood, can be used to create a variety of colors and effects, and are non-toxic and environmentally friendly.
- Drawbacks: Can be difficult to apply evenly, may require multiple coats for adequate coverage, can be prone to chipping or peeling, and may not be suitable for high-use items or outdoor use.

The best practices for achieving a smooth and durable finish

Achieving a smooth and durable finish is an essential step in woodworking that not only enhances the appearance of the final product but also helps to protect the wood from wear and tear. Here are some best practices for achieving a smooth and durable finish with natural products:

1. **Proper surface preparation:** Before applying any finish, it's important to prepare the wood

surface by sanding it to a smooth finish and removing any dust or debris. This ensures that the finish will adhere properly and provide an even coverage.

2. **Use the right applicator:** The choice of applicator depends on the type of finish being used. For oil-based finishes, a brush or cloth applicator is suitable, while for waxes and shellacs, a soft cloth is recommended.

3. **Apply thin coats:** Applying thin coats of finish allows for better penetration into the wood and prevents the buildup of excess finish, which can lead to drips and uneven coverage. It's better to apply several thin coats than a single thick coat.

4. **Allow adequate drying time**: Each type of finish has a specific drying time, which should be followed carefully. Rushing the drying process can result in a tacky finish that's prone to damage.

5. **Sand between coats:** Sanding between coats of finish not only helps to smooth out any imperfections but also allows for better adhesion of subsequent coats.

6. **Buff the final finish:** After the final coat has dried, buffing the surface with a soft cloth or polishing pad can help to achieve a smooth and glossy finish.

In addition to these best practices, it's important to choose natural finishes that are appropriate for the specific woodworking project. Oils, waxes, shellacs, and milk paint each have their benefits and drawbacks, so it's important to consider factors such as the desired level of protection, the type of wood being used, and the intended use of the finished product.

Overall, achieving a smooth and durable finish with natural products requires careful attention to detail, patience, and an understanding of the properties of different finishes. With proper technique and the right products, woodworkers can create beautiful and long-lasting finishes that showcase the natural beauty of the wood.

Chapter 9: Working with Salvaged and Reclaimed Wood

In recent years, there has been a growing trend towards sustainability and environmental consciousness in the woodworking industry. One of the ways woodworkers can contribute to this movement is by working with salvaged and reclaimed wood. Not only does this help reduce waste and preserve natural resources, but it also adds a unique character and history to a project. In this chapter, we will explore the benefits and challenges of working with salvaged and reclaimed wood, as well as practical tips and techniques for sourcing, preparing, and using these materials in woodworking projects.

Salvaged and Reclaimed Wood

Salvaged and reclaimed wood refer to wood that has been recovered from old buildings, barns, ships, or other structures and given new life as a building material. Salvaged wood may also come from trees that have fallen naturally or been removed for other purposes such as construction or roadwork.

Reclaimed wood, on the other hand, refers specifically to wood that has been removed from an old building or structure and then repurposed for a new project. Both salvaged and reclaimed wood have a distinct character and patina that cannot be replicated by new lumber, making them a popular choice among woodworkers and builders who value sustainability and unique aesthetics.

The Benefits of Working with Salvaged and Reclaimed Wood

Working with salvaged and reclaimed wood offers several benefits, including:

- **Environmental benefits:** Salvaged and reclaimed wood reduces the demand for newly harvested timber, which helps to preserve forests and reduces the carbon footprint associated with logging, transportation, and processing of new wood.

- **Unique character:** Salvaged and reclaimed wood often has a unique character and patina that cannot be replicated with new wood. The natural weathering and aging of salvaged and reclaimed wood give it a one-of-a-kind appearance that adds a distinct character to any woodworking project.

- **Historical significance:** Reclaimed wood may have a history that adds to its significance and value. It may have been salvaged from an old building or structure, giving it a connection to the past and a story to tell.

- **Strength and durability:** Salvaged and reclaimed wood may be denser and stronger than new wood because it has had time to mature and dry out. This can make it more durable and long-lasting, especially for outdoor projects.

- **Cost-effective:** Salvaged and reclaimed wood can be a cost-effective alternative to new wood, especially for large projects. It may also be less expensive to source and purchase salvaged and reclaimed wood than to purchase new, high-quality lumber.

Overall, working with salvaged and reclaimed wood is a sustainable and unique option for woodworkers who want to create beautiful and meaningful pieces while reducing their environmental impact.

The Challenges of Working with Salvaged and Reclaimed Wood

Working with salvaged and reclaimed wood can present unique challenges that differ from working with new wood. Some of the challenges include:

- **Limited availability:** Salvaged and reclaimed wood may be difficult to source, and the quantity and quality can vary depending on the source.

- **Wear and tear:** Salvaged and reclaimed wood often has signs of wear and tear, such as nail holes, dents, and scratches, which can make it more difficult to work with and require additional preparation.

- **Structural integrity:** Salvaged and reclaimed wood may have weakened structural integrity due to previous use, damage, or age, which can affect its strength and durability.

- **Inconsistency:** Salvaged and reclaimed wood may have inconsistencies in color, grain pattern, and texture due to its previous use and exposure to the elements.

- **Cost:** While salvaged and reclaimed wood can be more affordable than new wood in some cases, it can also be more expensive due to the sourcing and preparation required.

Despite these challenges, working with salvaged and reclaimed wood can be a rewarding experience that contributes to sustainability and adds character and uniqueness to a project.

The best Practices for Working with Salvaged and Reclaimed Wood

Here are some best practices for working with salvaged and reclaimed wood:

- **Inspection and preparation:** Before using salvaged or reclaimed wood, it's important to thoroughly inspect and prepare it for use. This may include removing nails, screws, and other hardware, and checking for any damage or rot that may need to be repaired.

- **Acclimation:** Salvaged and reclaimed wood may have a higher moisture content than new wood, so it's important to allow it to acclimate to the environment where it will be used before starting any projects. This can help prevent warping or shrinking after installation.

- **Planing and sanding:** Salvaged and reclaimed wood may have rough surfaces or irregularities, so it's important to plane and sand it properly to achieve a smooth and consistent surface. This can also help to reveal the natural beauty of the wood.

- **Finishing:** When finishing salvaged or reclaimed wood, it's important to choose a finish that will enhance its natural beauty and protect it from damage. This may include natural oils or waxes, or low-VOC (volatile organic compound) finishes.

- **Safety:** Salvaged and reclaimed wood may contain lead paint, nails, or other hazards, so it's important to take proper safety precautions when working with it. This may include wearing gloves, a dust mask, and safety goggles, and properly disposing of any hazardous materials.

By following these best practices, woodworkers can ensure that their salvaged and reclaimed wood projects are not only beautiful but also safe and durable.

Some Practical Tips and Techniques

Sure, here are some practical tips and techniques for working with salvaged and reclaimed wood:

Sourcing:
- Look for local sources such as salvage yards, old barns, and demolished buildings.

- Use online resources such as Craigslist, Facebook Marketplace, and online salvage stores.
- Always inspect the wood for rot, insect infestations, and other damage before purchasing.

Preparation:
- Remove any nails, screws, or other hardware from the wood.
- Clean the wood thoroughly with a wire brush, sandpaper, or a planer.
- Check for any hidden defects, such as knots or splits, and cut them out or work around them as necessary.

Usage:
- Choose a woodworking project that highlights the unique character and features of the salvaged wood.
- Consider using the wood in combination with new materials, such as metal or glass, to create a modern aesthetic.
- Be mindful of the wood's inherent weaknesses and strengths, and adjust your woodworking techniques accordingly.

Finishing:
- Use finishes that enhance the natural beauty of the wood, such as oils or waxes.
- Avoid using harsh chemicals or solvents that could damage the wood.
- Consider using a sealer or stain to protect the wood from moisture and other environmental factors.

Overall, working with salvaged and reclaimed wood requires patience, creativity, and a willingness to adapt to the unique qualities of each piece. With proper preparation and technique, these materials can add character and depth to any woodworking project while also promoting sustainability and environmental consciousness.

Section 4: Sustainable Wood Projects

- Chapter 10: The Different Kinds and Forms of wood crafts
- Chapter 11: Building Furniture with a Sustainable Mindset
- Chapter 12: Crafting Wooden Utensils and Kitchenware
- Chapter 13: Sustainable Woodworking for Home Improvement Projects

Chapter 10: The Different Kinds and Forms of wood crafts

Woodworking is a vast field that encompasses many different types and forms of crafts. From carving to furniture-making, there are many ways to work with wood to create beautiful and functional pieces. In this chapter, we will explore the different kinds and forms of wood crafts, including their history and cultural significance. We will also look at the tools and techniques used in each craft and provide examples of famous works in each category. Whether you are a seasoned woodworker or just starting out, this chapter will provide valuable insights into the world of wood crafts.

Kinds and Forms of Woodworking

Woodworking is a broad category of crafts that encompasses many different kinds and forms of woodworking. Here are some of the most common:

- **Carpentry**: Carpentry is the oldest form of woodworking and is the foundation for most other forms of woodworking. It involves the construction of buildings, furniture, and other objects using primarily hand tools..
- **Cabinetry**: Cabinetry is a form of woodworking that focuses on the construction of cabinets, which are typically used in kitchens and

bathrooms. It involves the use of precision tools and techniques to create high-quality, functional cabinets.

- **Woodturning**: Woodturning is the art of turning a piece of wood on a lathe to create a symmetrical object, such as a bowl, vase, or spindle. It is a highly skilled craft that requires a deep understanding of wood grain and the use of specialized tools.

- **Wood carving:** Wood carving is the art of carving intricate designs into a piece of wood using hand tools. It is a highly skilled craft that requires patience and precision.

- **Wood burning**: Wood burning, also known as pyrography, is the art of burning designs into a piece of wood using a heated tool. It is a versatile craft that can be used to create a wide range of designs, from simple patterns to highly detailed portraits.

- **Scroll sawing:** Scroll sawing involves cutting intricate patterns into thin pieces of wood using a specialized saw.

- **Marquetry**: Marquetry is the art of using different types and colors of wood veneers to create intricate designs and patterns. It is a highly skilled craft that requires a deep understanding of wood grain and the use of precision tools.

- **Intarsia**: Intarsia is a form of woodworking that involves the use of different types and colors of wood to create a three-dimensional image. It is a highly skilled craft that requires a deep understanding of wood grain and the use of precision tools.
- **Woodworking for construction:** Building structures and other practical items such as sheds, decks, and fences using wood
- **Woodworking for art and decoration:** Creating decorative items such as picture frames, wall hangings, and other crafts using various woodworking techniques.

Throughout history, different cultures have developed their own unique styles of woodworking. For example, in Japan, there is a long tradition of fine woodworking that emphasizes simplicity, elegance, and attention to detail. In Europe, there is a tradition of ornate, decorative woodworking, with intricate carvings and marquetry designs. In North America, there is a long tradition of rustic woodworking, with a focus on using natural materials and creating functional, durable objects. Overall, woodworking is a rich and diverse craft with a long and fascinating history.

Carpentry

Carpentry is one of the oldest and most essential crafts in human history. Its roots can be traced back to ancient Egypt, where skilled craftsmen used chisels and saws to carve intricate details into wooden furniture, statues, and buildings. In medieval Europe, carpenters played a crucial role in constructing castles, cathedrals, and other monumental structures that still stand today.

Carpentry involves working with wood to create structures, furniture, and decorative objects. This craft requires a variety of specialized tools, including saws, chisels, hammers, drills, planes, and measuring devices. The techniques used in carpentry vary depending on the project, but often involve cutting, shaping, and joining pieces of wood to form a cohesive whole.

Over the centuries, carpentry has developed into a highly specialized field with a wide range of applications. Some carpenters specialize in creating custom furniture, while others work on large-scale construction projects like houses and commercial buildings. In recent years, there has been a growing interest in using sustainable and reclaimed wood in carpentry projects, as well as in incorporating modern technologies like 3D printing and computer-aided design (CAD).

Examples of famous works in carpentry include the intricate carvings and sculptures found in Gothic cathedrals like Notre-Dame de Paris and the furniture designs of masters like Gustav Stickley and Charles and Ray Eames. Even today, carpentry continues to be an important and valuable craft, whether you are a seasoned woodworker or just starting out. With the right tools, techniques, and materials, anyone can create beautiful and functional objects from wood.

Cabinetry

Cabinetry is a branch of woodworking that involves building furniture pieces such as cabinets, shelves, and other storage units. The history of cabinetry can be traced back to ancient times when people began constructing furniture for functional purposes. However, cabinetry as an art form began to flourish during the Renaissance period in Europe when cabinets were crafted with intricate designs and decorations.

Cabinetry requires a set of specialized tools and techniques that differ from traditional woodworking. Some of the essential tools used in cabinetry include saws, routers, sanders, and drills. These tools are used to shape, cut, and join pieces of wood to create furniture pieces with precise measurements and angles.

One of the most popular cabinetry techniques is the use of dovetail joints, which provide a strong and durable connection between two pieces of wood. Other techniques used in cabinetry include mortise and tenon joints, tongue and groove joints, and rabbet joints.

Cabinetry has been used to create some of the most famous works of art and furniture throughout history. For example, the Palace of Versailles in France is known for its elaborate and intricate cabinetry designs, which were created by skilled artisans during the 17th and 18th centuries. In the United States, cabinet makers such as Thomas Seymour and Duncan Phyfe were renowned for their cabinetry pieces during the early 19th century.

Cabinetry can be a rewarding craft for both seasoned woodworkers and beginners. With the right tools and techniques, anyone can create functional and beautiful furniture pieces that can last for generations.

Woodturning

Woodturning is a form of woodworking that involves shaping wood using a lathe, a machine that spins a piece of wood while a craftsman uses various cutting tools to shape it into a desired form. The history of woodturning can be traced back to ancient Egypt and Rome, where lathes were used to turn objects such as table legs and bowls. In medieval Europe, woodturning became an important craft, with artisans producing elaborate wooden objects such as chalices, candlesticks, and chess pieces.

Today, woodturning is a popular hobby and a respected craft. The tools and techniques used in woodturning have evolved over time, but the basic principles remain the same. The most common tools used in woodturning include gouges, skews, chisels, and parting tools. These tools are used to remove wood from the spinning piece, creating various shapes and contours.

One of the unique aspects of woodturning is the ability to create objects that are both functional and beautiful. Examples of famous works in woodturning include wooden bowls, vases, and ornaments, as well as turned furniture components such as table legs and chair spindles. Notable woodturners throughout history include Rude Osolnik, David Ellsworth, and Michael Hosaluk.

For those who are just starting out in woodturning, it is important to begin with the basics and gradually build skills and techniques. Safety is also a crucial consideration, as woodturning involves sharp tools and spinning wood. With practice and dedication, woodturning can be a rewarding and fulfilling craft for woodworkers of all levels of experience.

Wood carving

Wood carving is an ancient art form that involves the use of various tools to create intricate designs and sculptures out of wood. The history of wood carving dates back to prehistoric times, with evidence of carved objects found in various archaeological sites around the world. Throughout history, wood carving has been used for both functional and decorative purposes, with examples ranging from small household items to large architectural features.

The techniques and tools used in wood carving have evolved over time, with various styles and methods developed by different cultures around the world. Some of the most common tools used in wood carving include chisels, gouges, knives, and saws, as well as power tools such as rotary tools and chainsaws.

Wood carving is a highly skilled craft that requires a great deal of patience and attention to detail. The techniques used in wood carving can be complex, and mastering them takes time and practice. However, with the right tools and guidance, even novice woodworkers can learn to create beautiful and intricate carvings.

Some famous examples of wood carving include the intricate designs found on Gothic-style furniture, the detailed carvings of Native American totem poles, and the delicate filigree work of Chinese and Japanese wood carvings.

Wood carving can be a rewarding hobby for people of all skill levels, and there are many resources available for those looking to get started. Whether you are a seasoned woodworker or just starting out, learning the techniques and tools used in wood carving can be a fun and rewarding experience.

Wood burning

Wood burning, also known as pyrography, is a technique of creating decorative designs on wood using a heated tool. The history of wood burning can be traced back to ancient Egypt and China, where it was used to create intricate designs on furniture and other wooden objects. The technique gained popularity in Europe during the Victorian era, where it was used to decorate household items such as picture frames, boxes, and furniture.

Wood burning requires specialized tools, including a heated pen or wire, as well as various tips for creating different patterns and textures. The pen is heated by either electricity or butane, and the tip is used to burn the design into the wood.

The technique of wood burning involves using controlled heat to burn designs into the surface of the wood. This requires precision and patience, as the artist must be able to control the temperature of the pen and the pressure applied to the wood to create the desired effect. Different types of wood can be used for wood burning, with hardwoods such as maple and birch being preferred due to their durability and ability to hold fine details.

Examples of famous works in wood burning include the intricately designed wooden boxes and decorative objects of the Victorian era, as well as contemporary works of art created by modern artists.

Wood burning can be enjoyed by woodworkers of all skill levels, from beginners to seasoned professionals. It is a versatile technique that can be used to create a wide range of decorative items, from intricate designs on furniture to personalized wooden gifts. However, it does require a steady hand and attention to detail to achieve the desired results.

Scroll sawing

Scroll sawing is a woodworking technique that involves cutting intricate designs in wood using a scroll saw. This craft has a rich history dating back to the 16th century when the first scroll saws were developed in Europe. The popularity of scroll sawing has continued to grow throughout the years, and it remains a popular hobby and art form today.

Tools commonly used in scroll sawing include a scroll saw, blades of various sizes and shapes, sandpaper, and a variety of clamps and vises to hold the wood in place during cutting. Techniques used in scroll sawing include fretwork, inlay work, and marquetry, which involve cutting and piecing together small pieces of wood to create intricate designs.

Famous works in scroll sawing include the detailed and intricate fretwork designs of Victorian-era furniture, as well as the whimsical and playful designs of modern scroll saw artists. Some notable scroll saw artists include Frank Droege, who specializes in creating intricate wildlife designs, and Gary MacKay, who creates detailed and lifelike portraits using the scroll saw.

Scroll sawing is a craft that can be enjoyed by both seasoned woodworkers and those who are just starting out. It is a great way to express creativity and create unique and intricate designs in wood. With the right tools, techniques, and practice, anyone can become skilled in the art of scroll sawing.

Marquetry

Marquetry is a woodworking technique that involves the use of veneers, or thin slices of wood, to create decorative patterns and designs on furniture, flooring, and other wooden surfaces. The history of marquetry can be traced back to ancient Egypt, where it was used to decorate the tombs of pharaohs. It later became popular in Europe during the Renaissance and Baroque periods, particularly in France and Italy.

The process of marquetry involves cutting and assembling small pieces of wood veneer into intricate patterns, which are then glued onto a larger wooden surface. A variety of tools and techniques are used in marquetry, including saws, knives, chisels, and sandpaper, as well as hot sand or metal plates for flattening and bending the veneer.

One famous example of marquetry is the "Salvator Mundi" cabinet, which was created by Italian artist Andrea del Verrocchio and his workshop in the late 15th century. The cabinet features intricate marquetry designs depicting scenes from the life of Christ, as well as animals and floral motifs.

Marquetry is a challenging woodworking technique that requires a high degree of skill and precision. It can be useful for both seasoned woodworkers and beginners who are looking to expand their skills and create decorative pieces of furniture or artwork.

Intarsia

Intarsia is a form of woodworking that involves creating pictures or designs by inlaying various shapes and pieces of wood into a larger wooden surface. It originated in the Middle East and was later popularized in Italy during the Renaissance period.

The term "intarsia" comes from the Italian word "intarsiare," which means to inlay. The technique involves using a variety of woods, each with different colors and textures, to create a mosaic-like effect.

Intarsia requires a set of specialized tools, including saws, chisels, and knives. The process involves creating a design on paper, then cutting out each individual piece of wood to fit the design. The pieces are then carefully fitted together and glued onto a base piece of wood.

Famous examples of intarsia can be seen in the intricate woodwork found in Italian cathedrals and palaces from the 14th and 15th centuries. In modern times, intarsia has remained a popular form of woodworking, often used in furniture making and decorative objects.

While intarsia can be a challenging technique to master, it can be a rewarding project for both seasoned woodworkers and those just starting out. With patience and attention to detail, stunning and intricate designs can be achieved.

Woodworking for construction

Woodworking for construction is the practice of using wood as a primary building material in construction projects, such as building homes, commercial buildings, and infrastructure. This type of woodworking has a long history, dating back to ancient civilizations like the Egyptians and Greeks who used wood in the construction of buildings, ships, and furniture.

In more recent history, woodworking for construction has been a vital part of the building industry. In the 19th and early 20th centuries, many houses and commercial buildings were constructed with wooden frames, and even today, wood remains a popular choice for construction due to its durability, versatility, and sustainability.

Tools commonly used in woodworking for construction include circular saws, power drills, hammers, chisels, and hand saws. Techniques used in this type of woodworking include framing, roofing, siding, and finishing, which involve measuring and cutting wood to fit specific spaces, and joining the pieces together using nails, screws, and glue.

Examples of famous works in this category include the timber framing of medieval European buildings, such as the cathedrals of Notre-Dame and Chartres, and the post-and-beam construction of traditional Japanese architecture, such as the Horyu-ji temple in Nara.

Woodworking for construction can be useful for both seasoned woodworkers and those just starting out, as it involves a combination of basic and advanced techniques and provides opportunities for creativity and problem-solving in building projects.

Woodworking for art and decoration

Woodworking for art and decoration has been practiced for centuries and has a rich history and cultural significance in many parts of the world. From creating intricate patterns and designs to carving sculptures and creating functional objects, woodworking has been used as a form of artistic expression and decoration.

In ancient Egypt, woodworking was used to create decorative objects such as furniture, jewelry boxes, and other intricate items. The ancient Greeks and Romans also used woodworking to create intricate carvings and decorative items for their homes and public buildings.

During the Renaissance period in Europe, woodworking became a popular art form, with artists using wood to create sculptures and elaborate furniture pieces. In Japan, woodworking has a long history and is often used to create traditional objects such as tea boxes, musical instruments, and furniture.

Today, woodworking for art and decoration remains popular and is practiced by many skilled artisans around the world. The techniques used in this type of woodworking can vary greatly depending on the specific project and desired outcome.

Tools commonly used in woodworking for art and decoration include chisels, saws, routers, sanders, and carving knives. Techniques such as carving, inlay, marquetry, and wood burning are often used to create intricate patterns and designs.

Famous works in woodworking for art and decoration include the carved wooden altarpieces of the German Renaissance, the marquetry works of the French cabinetmakers of the 18th century, and the intricate carvings of Chinese and Japanese woodworkers.

Whether you are a seasoned woodworker or just starting out, woodworking for art and decoration can be a rewarding and fulfilling craft. With dedication and practice, you can create beautiful and unique pieces that showcase your creativity and skill.

Chapter 11: Building Furniture with a Sustainable Mindset

As concern for the environment and sustainability grows, it is becoming increasingly important for woodworkers to approach their craft with a sustainable mindset. In this chapter, we will explore the ways in which woodworkers can build furniture that not only meets their functional and aesthetic needs but also considers the impact on the environment. From sourcing materials to choosing finishes, this chapter will provide practical guidance for woodworkers who want to create beautiful, functional, and sustainable furniture.

The Ways in which Woodworkers can Build Furniture

Woodworkers can build furniture with a sustainable mindset by using environmentally friendly materials and production methods. This includes using wood from sustainable sources, such as forests that are responsibly managed and harvested. Additionally, using reclaimed or salvaged wood can reduce the need for new resources.

Another way to build sustainable furniture is to use non-toxic finishes and adhesives. Traditional finishes such as lacquers and varnishes often contain harsh chemicals that are harmful to the environment and to human health. Using natural finishes like linseed oil, beeswax, or shellac can be a more sustainable option.

Designing furniture with durability in mind can also contribute to sustainability. Furniture that is well-made and built to last can reduce the need for frequent replacements, thus reducing waste.

In terms of production methods, woodworkers can reduce their environmental impact by using efficient machinery and tools that consume less energy. Additionally, reducing waste and recycling materials can also be effective in reducing the environmental impact of woodworking.

Overall, building furniture with a sustainable mindset involves considering the entire lifecycle of the product, from material sourcing to production to eventual disposal. By using environmentally friendly materials and methods, woodworkers can create furniture that not only meets their needs but also contributes to a more sustainable future.

Woodworkers can build furniture that is both functional and environmentally responsible by following a few key principles. Here are some ways in which woodworkers can consider the impact on the environment when building furniture:

- **Sourcing Sustainable Materials:** One of the most important steps in building environmentally responsible furniture is to source wood from sustainable forests. This means choosing wood that has been certified by organizations such as the Forest Stewardship Council (FSC) or the Sustainable Forestry Initiative (SFI) which ensures that the wood is harvested responsibly and that the forest is managed sustainably.

Alternatively, woodworkers can also source wood from reclaimed or salvaged sources, reducing the demand for newly harvested wood.

- **Minimizing Waste:** Woodworkers can also reduce their environmental impact by minimizing waste in their furniture-making process. This can be achieved by carefully planning cuts and using every part of the wood, including scraps and offcuts. Additionally, choosing joinery techniques that require less material and produce less waste can also help.

- **Choosing Eco-Friendly Finishes:** When finishing furniture, woodworkers can choose eco-friendly finishes such as natural oils, waxes, or water-based finishes that do not contain harmful chemicals. These finishes are safer for both the environment and the woodworker.

- **Considering the Product Life Cycle:** Woodworkers can also consider the entire lifecycle of their furniture when building it. This means designing furniture that is built to last, can be repaired if necessary, and can be easily disassembled and recycled at the end of its life.

- **Reducing Energy Consumption:** Finally, woodworkers can reduce their environmental impact by reducing energy consumption in their workshops. This can be achieved by using energy-efficient equipment and tools, as well as optimizing workspace layout and natural lighting to reduce the need for artificial lighting.

By following these principles, woodworkers can build furniture that not only meets their functional and aesthetic needs but also considers the impact on the environment.

Here are some practical guidance for woodworkers who want to create beautiful, functional, and sustainable furniture:

- Choose sustainably sourced wood: Look for wood that has been certified by organizations such as the Forest Stewardship Council (FSC) or the Sustainable Forestry Initiative (SFI). These organizations ensure that the wood is harvested in an environmentally responsible manner.

- Use reclaimed or salvaged wood: Using wood that has already been harvested and processed reduces the demand for new trees to be cut down.
- Consider the lifespan of the furniture: Build furniture that is designed to last for generations, rather than something that will need to be replaced in a few years.

- Avoid toxic finishes: Look for finishes that are non-toxic and environmentally friendly. For example, natural oils and waxes are a good alternative to chemical-laden finishes.

- Use energy-efficient tools: Choose tools that are energy efficient and have a minimal impact on the environment. For example, consider using hand tools instead of power tools when possible.

- Practice waste reduction: Reduce waste by using scraps and offcuts for smaller projects or for kindling. Look for ways to recycle or repurpose leftover materials.

- Collaborate with other artisans: Work with other artisans to source materials, share resources, and promote sustainable practices within the woodworking community.

By following these guidelines, woodworkers can create beautiful and functional furniture that also considers the impact on the environment.

The Art of Creating Handmade Wooden Furniture

Creating handmade wooden furniture is a craft that has been practiced for centuries, and is still popular today. Whether you are an experienced woodworker or just starting out, there are a few key techniques and tools you need to know to create beautiful and functional pieces.

One of the first steps in creating wooden furniture is choosing the right wood. Different types of wood have different characteristics, such as hardness, grain pattern, and color. Some of the most popular woods used in furniture making include oak, maple, cherry, and walnut, but there are many other options available depending on the desired look and function of the piece.

Once you have selected your wood, it's time to plan and design your furniture. This can involve creating detailed drawings or using computer-aided design (CAD) software to visualize the piece before you begin cutting and shaping the wood.

The next step is to use various tools and techniques to cut and shape the wood. This can include hand tools such as saws, chisels, and planes, as well as power tools like table saws, routers, and sanders. Some woodworkers also use carving tools to create intricate designs or decorative details on their furniture.

Joinery is another Important aspect of furniture making. This involves connecting pieces of wood together in a way that is both strong and aesthetically pleasing. There are many different types of joinery techniques, including mortise and tenon, dovetail, and biscuit joinery.

Once the furniture is assembled, it's time to finish the wood. This can involve sanding the surface to create a smooth texture, staining or dyeing the wood to add color, and applying a protective finish such as oil or varnish to help protect the wood from wear and tear.

Creating handmade wooden furniture is a rewarding and fulfilling craft that allows you to create functional pieces that can last for generations. Whether you are creating a simple chair or an intricate cabinet, there are many techniques and tools to master along the way.

The Techniques and Tools needed to Craft Wooden Furniture

Crafting wooden furniture requires a variety of tools and techniques, some of which are more specialized than others. Here are some of the essential tools and techniques needed to create handmade wooden furniture:

- **Measuring and marking tools:** To ensure accuracy in your furniture construction, you will need measuring and marking tools like rulers, squares, and marking gauges.

- **Cutting tools:** A range of cutting tools will be necessary for furniture making, including hand saws, power saws, chisels, and planes.

- **Joinery techniques**: Joinery refers to the methods used to connect different pieces of wood together. There are many different techniques for joining wood, including mortise and tenon, dovetail, and biscuit joinery.

- **Shaping and smoothing tools:** To create curves, contours, and smooth surfaces in your furniture, you will need shaping and smoothing tools like rasps, files, and sandpaper.

- **Finishing techniques:** The finishing process involves sanding, staining, and sealing the wood to protect it and enhance its appearance.

When it comes to the type of wood used in furniture making, there are many options to choose from. Some of the most popular woods for furniture making include:

1. Oak: Oak is a strong and durable hardwood that is known for its attractive grain patterns.

2. Maple: Maple is a dense and durable hardwood that is commonly used in furniture making due to its strength and stability.

3. Cherry: Cherry is a hardwood with a distinctive reddish-brown color and a fine grain pattern.

4. Walnut: Walnut is a popular hardwood with a rich, dark color and a straight, open grain.

5. Mahogany: Mahogany is a hardwood that is valued for its deep, rich color and attractive grain patterns.

Each type of wood has its own benefits and drawbacks, and the choice of wood will depend on the specific requirements of the furniture being made.

Overall, crafting handmade wooden furniture requires a combination of skill, patience, and attention to detail, as well as a range of specialized tools and techniques. With the right tools and materials, however, anyone can learn to create beautiful and functional pieces of furniture that will last for generations.

The most Popular Types of Wood for Furniture

There are many types of wood that are commonly used in furniture making, each with its own unique properties and characteristics. Some of the most popular types of wood for furniture include:

- Oak: Oak is a strong, durable wood that is commonly used in furniture making. It has a distinctive grain pattern and can be stained in a variety of colors.

- Walnut: Walnut is a hardwood that is known for its rich, dark color and attractive grain patterns. It is often used in high-end furniture pieces.

- Maple: Maple is a light-colored wood that is prized for its hardness and durability. It is often used in kitchen cabinets and other high-traffic areas.

- Cherry: Cherry wood is known for its warm, reddish-brown color and fine grain pattern. It is often used in traditional-style furniture pieces.

- Mahogany: Mahogany is a tropical hardwood that is prized for its deep, rich color and durability. It is often used in high-end furniture pieces and musical instruments.

- Pine: Pine is a softwood that is commonly used in furniture making. It is lightweight and has a pale, yellowish color.

- Teak: Teak is a tropical hardwood that is known for its durability and resistance to water and insects. It is often used in outdoor furniture pieces.

- Cedar: Cedar is a softwood that is prized for its natural resistance to insects and decay. It is often used in outdoor furniture and closet linings.

These are just a few of the most popular types of wood used in furniture making. The choice of wood will depend on the intended use of the furniture piece, as well as the desired aesthetic and budget.

Chapter 12: Crafting Wooden Utensils and Kitchenware

This chapter will delve into the art of creating handmade wooden utensils and kitchenware. From spoons and spatulas to cutting boards and bowls, wooden kitchenware has been a staple in households for centuries. In recent years, the popularity of handmade wooden kitchenware has surged as people seek more sustainable and natural alternatives to plastic and metal utensils.

Crafting wooden kitchenware is not only a functional skill but also a creative one. It requires attention to detail, an understanding of wood properties, and an eye for design. This chapter will explore the history and cultural significance of wooden kitchenware, as well as the tools, materials, and techniques used to create beautiful and functional pieces. Whether you are a seasoned woodworker or a beginner looking to explore a new craft, this chapter will provide practical guidance and inspiration for crafting your own handmade wooden utensils and kitchenware.

The Art of Creating Handmade Wooden Utensils and Kitchenware

The art of creating handmade wooden utensils and kitchenware is a timeless craft that has been passed down for generations. From spoons and spatulas to bowls and cutting boards, wooden kitchenware not only serves its functional purpose but also adds a touch of warmth and beauty to any kitchen. Crafting these items by hand requires patience, skill, and attention to detail.

The Techniques and Tools needed to Craft Wooden Utensils and Kitchenware

Crafting wooden utensils and kitchenware requires a few essential tools and techniques. Here are some of the most common ones:

- **Hand saw:** A hand saw is used to cut the wood into the desired shape and size. Choose a saw with a fine-toothed blade for more precise cuts.

- **Carving knives:** A set of carving knives with different blade shapes and sizes is necessary for carving and shaping the wood. They are used to make intricate cuts and details.

- **Sandpaper:** Sandpaper is used to smooth the surface of the wood and remove any rough edges or splinters.

- **Drill:** A drill is used to create holes in the wood for attaching handles or for other purposes.

- **Lathe:** A lathe is a specialized tool used to turn wood and shape it into a particular form. It is commonly used for making bowls, spoons, and other rounded objects.

- Chisels: Chisels are used to remove wood and shape the wood to the desired form. They come in various sizes and shapes.

- Wood burning tool: A wood burning tool is used to create decorative designs or patterns on the wooden surface.

- When working with wood, it's important to take safety precautions and wear appropriate safety gear such as eye protection, dust masks, and gloves.

To craft wooden utensils and kitchenware, follow these steps:

Choose the wood: Select a hardwood that is durable and non-toxic, such as maple, cherry, or walnut.

- **Cut the wood:** Use a hand saw to cut the wood into the desired size and shape.

- **Shape the wood:** Use carving knives, chisels, and a lathe to shape the wood into the desired form. Sand the surface to remove any rough spots.

- **Finish the wood:** Apply food-safe finishes such as mineral oil or beeswax to protect the wood and enhance its natural beauty.

- **Optional:** Use a wood burning tool to add decorative designs or patterns to the surface.

By following these steps and using the appropriate tools and techniques, woodworkers can create beautiful and functional wooden utensils and kitchenware that can last for generations.

Here is a step-by-step guide for creating handmade wooden utensils and kitchenware:

- **Select the wood:** Choose a type of wood that is suitable for kitchenware and utensils such as hard maple, cherry, or walnut.

- **Prepare the wood:** Cut the wood to the desired length and thickness. Use a planer to even out the surface and sandpaper to smooth it out.

- **Design and shape**: Sketch out the design of the utensil or kitchenware you want to create. Use a band saw or a scroll saw to cut out the shape. You can use chisels, carving knives, or a lathe to create the desired shape and texture.

- **Sand and smooth:** Use sandpaper of varying grits to smooth out the surface of the utensil or kitchenware. Start with a lower grit (80-100) and move up to higher grits (200-400) until the surface is smooth.

- **Add finish:** Choose a food-safe finish such as mineral oil or beeswax to protect the wood and enhance its natural beauty. Apply the finish with a clean cloth, following the manufacturer's instructions.

- **Allow to dry:** Let the utensil or kitchenware dry completely before using it. This may take a few hours or overnight depending on the type of finish used.

- **Maintenance**: Wooden utensils and kitchenware need to be well-maintained to ensure their longevity. Wash them with mild soap and warm water, and dry them thoroughly after use. Apply a food-safe oil or wax occasionally to keep the wood moisturized.

By following these steps, you can create beautiful and functional wooden utensils and kitchenware that will add a personal touch to your cooking and dining experiences.

The most Popular Types of Wood for utensils and kitchenware

There are several types of wood that are suitable for crafting wooden utensils and kitchenware. Some of the most popular types of wood include:

- **Hardwoods:** Hardwoods such as maple, cherry, and walnut are great for crafting kitchenware. These woods are dense and durable, making them ideal for cutting boards, utensils, and bowls. They are also resistant to water and can withstand heavy use.

- **Softwoods:** Softwoods such as pine, cedar, and spruce are softer and less dense than hardwoods, making them ideal for carving and shaping. These woods are great for making spoons, spatulas, and other utensils that require a lot of shaping and carving.

- **Exotic woods:** Exotic woods such as ebony, rosewood, and teak are prized for their beauty and durability. They are often used to make high-end cutting boards and utensils, but can be expensive and difficult to source.

When choosing a wood for your project, consider the following factors:

- **Durability:** The wood should be durable enough to withstand regular use and exposure to moisture.

- **Grain:** The grain of the wood should be tight and even, with few knots or irregularities.

- **Hardness:** The hardness of the wood will affect how easy it is to carve and shape.

- **Sustainability:** Consider using sustainably sourced wood to minimize the environmental impact of your project.

It's important to note that some woods can be toxic when used in cooking or eating utensils. For example, woods such as yew, elderberry, and oleander should not be used for kitchenware. Always do your research before using a new type of wood in your project.

In terms of drawbacks, some types of wood can be expensive or difficult to source, while others may require special tools or techniques to work with. It's also important to properly maintain and care for wooden kitchenware to prevent bacteria growth and ensure its longevity.

Finishing is an important step in the process of crafting wooden utensils and kitchenware. Not only does it protect the wood from damage and wear, but it also enhances the natural beauty of the wood and can even improve its function. Here are some common finishing techniques that woodworkers use:

- **Oil finishes:** One of the simplest and most effective ways to finish wooden utensils and kitchenware is with an oil finish. This involves applying a food-safe oil, such as mineral oil or walnut oil, to the wood surface. The oil penetrates the wood, protecting it from moisture and staining, while also bringing out its natural beauty.

- **Beeswax finishes:** Beeswax is another natural material that can be used to finish wooden utensils and kitchenware. A mixture of melted beeswax and mineral oil is brushed onto the wood and then buffed with a cloth to create a smooth, protective surface.

- **Varnish or lacquer finishes:** For a more durable finish, varnish or lacquer can be applied to the wood surface. These finishes create a hard, protective layer on top of the wood, but they can be less food-safe than oil or wax finishes.

- **Shellac finishes:** Shellac is a natural resin that can be dissolved in alcohol to create a finish that is both durable and food-safe. It dries quickly and can be applied in thin layers to build up a protective surface.

- **Burnishing:** Burnishing involves rubbing the wood surface with a smooth, hard object, such as a polished stone or a metal spoon. This compresses the wood fibers and creates a smooth, shiny surface that is also more resistant to moisture.

When choosing a finishing technique, it's important to consider both the function and aesthetics of the piece, as well as the level of protection needed for the intended use. Additionally, it's important to use materials that are safe for food contact and to follow proper safety precautions when applying finishes.

Chapter 13: Sustainable Woodworking for Home Improvement Projects

In recent years, there has been a growing interest in sustainable living and environmentally conscious practices. This has led many homeowners to seek out sustainable solutions for their home improvement projects, including the use of sustainable wood products. In this chapter, we will explore the concept of sustainable woodworking for home improvement projects and provide practical guidance for those looking to undertake such projects.

We will examine the benefits of sustainable woodworking, including the positive impact it can have on the environment, as well as the economic and health benefits of using sustainable materials. We will also discuss the various certification systems that exist to help consumers identify sustainable wood products and the importance of supporting sustainable forestry practices.

Additionally, we will provide practical guidance on how to incorporate sustainable woodworking practices into home improvement projects. This will include tips on choosing sustainable materials, reducing waste, and minimizing the environmental impact of woodworking projects. We will also explore the use of eco-friendly finishes and other sustainable techniques that can be used to improve the longevity and sustainability of home improvement projects.

Whether you are a seasoned woodworker or a DIY enthusiast looking to embark on a sustainable home improvement project, this chapter will provide valuable insights and guidance to help you achieve your goals while minimizing your environmental impact.

The Concept of Sustainable Woodworking for Home Improvement Projects

Sustainable woodworking for home improvement projects is the practice of using environmentally friendly and socially responsible methods and materials to create functional and aesthetically pleasing additions to a home. This approach to woodworking involves considering the full lifecycle of a project, from the sourcing of materials to the disposal or repurposing of waste.

One important aspect of sustainable woodworking is using responsibly sourced wood. This means using wood that has been harvested in a way that ensures the continued health and productivity of the forest ecosystem, as well as the rights and well-being of workers and local communities. Sustainable wood sources may include forests certified by organizations such as the Forest Stewardship Council (FSC) or wood salvaged from old structures or urban trees.

Another key component of sustainable woodworking is reducing waste by maximizing the use of materials. This can involve carefully planning projects to minimize scrap, using efficient cutting methods, and repurposing or recycling wood scraps. For example, leftover wood from one project can be used to create smaller items such as cutting boards or coasters.

In addition to responsible sourcing and waste reduction, sustainable woodworking also involves minimizing the environmental impact of finishing materials. This can include using natural oils and waxes instead of synthetic finishes that contain harmful chemicals. It can also involve choosing finishes that are water-based and low in volatile organic compounds (VOCs), which can be harmful to both the environment and human health.

Overall, sustainable woodworking for home improvement projects is about creating beautiful and functional additions to a home while minimizing the negative impact on the environment and promoting responsible and ethical practices. By taking a sustainable approach to woodworking, we can create a more sustainable future for both our homes and our planet.

If you are looking to undertake sustainable woodworking projects for home improvement, here are some practical guidelines that can help:

1. **Choose sustainable materials:** Opt for materials that are sourced responsibly, such as FSC-certified wood or reclaimed wood from salvaged sources. Avoid materials that contribute to deforestation, such as tropical hardwoods.

2. **Use non-toxic finishes**: Choose finishes that are low-VOC or natural, such as linseed oil, beeswax, or milk paint. These finishes are not only better for the environment but also for your health.

3. **Design for durability:** Create furniture or home improvement projects that are built to last. Choose sturdy joinery techniques and materials that can withstand wear and tear over time.

4. **Reduce waste:** Try to minimize waste by using every part of the wood that you can. Use scraps for smaller projects, or consider donating them to local woodworking schools or community centers.

5. **Energy efficiency:** Consider energy-efficient design elements when building your projects. For example, use materials that have good insulating properties, such as wood, and design windows and doors that prevent air leakage.

6. **Repair and repurpose:** Instead of throwing away old furniture or materials, repair or repurpose them. This not only reduces waste but also gives new life to old pieces.

By following these guidelines, you can create beautiful and functional home improvement projects while minimizing your impact on the environment.

The Benefits of Sustainable Woodworking

Sustainable woodworking has numerous benefits, including environmental, economic, and health benefits. Here are some of the main advantages:

- **Environmental Benefits:** Sustainable woodworking helps protect the environment by using materials that are responsibly sourced, renewable, and biodegradable. This reduces the impact of deforestation and promotes biodiversity.

- **Economic Benefits:** Sustainable woodworking supports local economies by using locally sourced materials, supporting small businesses, and creating jobs. This helps to build more resilient and self-sufficient communities.

- **Health Benefits:** Sustainable woodworking can improve indoor air quality by using materials that are free of harmful chemicals and pollutants. This can help to reduce the risk of respiratory problems and other health issues.

- **Long-term Cost Savings:** Sustainable woodworking can lead to long-term cost savings, as using high-quality, durable materials means that projects will require less maintenance and replacement over time.

- **Aesthetic Benefits:** Sustainable woodworking can create beautiful, unique, and high-quality products that are aesthetically pleasing and add value to homes and buildings.

To undertake sustainable woodworking projects, here are some practical guidelines to follow:

- **Choose sustainably sourced materials:** Look for wood that has been certified by reputable organizations such as the Forest Stewardship Council (FSC) or the Sustainable Forestry Initiative (SFI).

- **Use reclaimed or salvaged wood:** Salvaged wood can be a great source of high-quality material that would otherwise go to waste. It also has unique character and history that can add value to a project.

- **Use non-toxic finishes:** Choose finishes that are low in volatile organic compounds (VOCs) to reduce indoor air pollution and protect the health of those who use the space.

- **Minimize waste**: Plan your project carefully to minimize waste and use scraps for other projects or as firewood.

- **Choose energy-efficient tools:** Look for tools that are energy efficient and use renewable sources of energy such as solar power.

By following these guidelines, woodworkers can create beautiful, functional, and sustainable home improvement projects that benefit both the environment and the community.

The Various Certification Systems

There are various certification systems that exist to help consumers identify sustainable wood products. These certification systems ensure that the wood products come from responsibly managed forests that meet certain environmental, social, and economic standards. Some of the most recognized certification systems include the Forest Stewardship Council (FSC), the Programme for the Endorsement of Forest Certification (PEFC), and the Sustainable Forestry Initiative (SFI).

The Forest Stewardship Council (FSC) is one of the most recognized certification systems for sustainable forestry. It is an international organization that works to promote responsible forestry practices worldwide. The FSC certification ensures that the wood products come from forests that are managed to meet certain environmental, social, and economic standards. These standards include protecting biodiversity, maintaining the health and vitality of the forest, respecting the rights of workers and local communities, and promoting responsible forest management.

The Programme for the Endorsement of Forest Certification (PEFC) is another well-known certification system. It is an international non-profit organization that works to promote sustainable forest management practices worldwide. The PEFC certification ensures that the wood products come from forests that are managed to meet certain environmental, social, and economic standards. These standards include protecting biodiversity, maintaining the health and vitality of the forest, respecting the rights of workers and local communities, and promoting responsible forest management.

The Sustainable Forestry Initiative (SFI) is a North American certification system that works to promote sustainable forest management practices in the United States and Canada. The SFI certification ensures that the wood products come from forests that are managed to meet certain environmental, social, and economic standards. These standards include protecting biodiversity, maintaining the health and vitality of the forest, respecting the rights of workers and local communities, and promoting responsible forest management.

Supporting sustainable forestry practices is important because it helps to ensure that forests are managed in a way that balances economic, environmental, and social considerations. Sustainable forestry practices can help to protect wildlife habitats, maintain soil and water quality, and mitigate climate change by sequestering carbon. In addition, supporting sustainable forestry practices can also have economic benefits by creating jobs in forestry and related industries. By choosing products that are certified as sustainable, consumers can help to promote responsible forest management practices and protect the health and

Practical Guidance on how to Incorporate Sustainable Woodworking Practices into Home Improvement Projects

Here are some practical tips on how to incorporate sustainable woodworking practices into home improvement projects:

- **Use reclaimed or salvaged wood:** Reclaimed wood can be salvaged from old buildings, barns, or other sources and can be repurposed for use in new home improvement projects. This not only saves resources but also adds character and uniqueness to the project.

- **Choose FSC-certified wood:** The Forest Stewardship Council (FSC) is an international certification system that ensures the wood used in a project is harvested sustainably. Look for FSC-certified wood products to ensure that the wood is sourced responsibly.

- **Avoid using exotic or endangered wood species:** Some wood species are endangered or threatened, and their use can contribute to deforestation and habitat loss. Instead, opt for locally sourced wood species or those that are abundant and sustainably managed.

- **Use non-toxic finishes:** Traditional wood finishes can release volatile organic compounds (VOCs) that are harmful to human health and the environment. Look for non-toxic finishes that are water-based, low-VOC, or natural alternatives like tung oil or beeswax.

- **Plan your cuts and minimize waste**: Plan your cuts carefully to minimize waste and maximize the use of your wood. Consider repurposing scraps for smaller projects or using them for kindling.

- **Consider alternative materials:** Consider alternative materials like bamboo, cork, or recycled materials like plastic or metal when appropriate. These materials can be eco-friendly, durable, and stylish.

By incorporating these practices into your home improvement projects, you can help reduce your impact on the environment while creating beautiful and functional spaces.

Here are some practical tips on how to incorporate sustainable wood products into home improvement projects:

1. **Look for certified sustainable wood products:** When purchasing wood products, look for labels or certifications such as the Forest Stewardship Council (FSC) or the Sustainable Forestry Initiative (SFI). These certifications ensure that the wood has been harvested in a sustainable manner.

2. **Use reclaimed wood:** Instead of buying new wood, consider using reclaimed wood for your home improvement projects. Reclaimed wood is salvaged from old buildings, barns, or other structures and can add character and charm to your project while reducing the demand for new wood.

3. **Use engineered wood products:** Engineered wood products such as laminated veneer lumber (LVL) and oriented strand board (OSB) are made from small pieces of wood that are glued and pressed together. They are strong and stable and can be used in place of solid wood in many applications.

4. **Use bamboo:** Bamboo is a fast-growing and renewable resource that can be used as an alternative to traditional hardwoods. It is also strong and durable, making it a good choice for home improvement projects.

5. **Use finishes that are eco-friendly:** Choose finishes that are low-VOC (volatile organic compound) or zero-VOC to reduce harmful emissions. Water-based finishes are also a good choice as they are easier to clean up and produce fewer harmful fumes.

By incorporating sustainable wood products into your home improvement projects, you can help to reduce the impact on the environment while creating a beautiful and functional space.

Here are some tips on how to incorporate sustainable woodworking practices into home improvement projects:

- Choose sustainable wood products: Look for wood that is certified by organizations like the Forest Stewardship Council (FSC) or the Sustainable Forestry Initiative (SFI). These organizations ensure that the wood comes from well-managed forests that are harvested in an environmentally responsible way.

- Use reclaimed wood: Instead of using newly harvested wood, consider using reclaimed wood from old buildings or furniture. This not only reduces waste but also gives a unique character to your project.

- Avoid exotic and endangered wood species: Many exotic wood species are endangered due to over-harvesting, and their use can contribute to deforestation. Stick to locally available wood species that are sustainably sourced.

- Reduce waste: Plan your project carefully to minimize waste. Use scraps for smaller projects or donate them to local woodworking programs or schools.

- Use non-toxic finishes: Traditional wood finishes often contain toxic chemicals that can be harmful to the environment and your health. Look for non-toxic and eco-friendly finishes that

- are water-based and contain low or zero volatile organic compounds (VOCs).
-
- Consider energy efficiency: If you're building something like cabinets or shelving, consider designing them to be energy-efficient by incorporating LED lighting or other energy-efficient features.

By incorporating these sustainable woodworking practices into your home improvement projects, you can help reduce your impact on the environment while still enjoying the beauty and functionality of handmade woodwork.

The use of Eco-Friendly Finishes and other Sustainable Techniques

Eco-friendly finishes and sustainable techniques can play a significant role in the longevity and sustainability of home improvement projects. Here are some options to consider:

- **Natural oils and waxes:** Instead of synthetic varnishes and lacquers, natural oils and waxes such as tung oil, linseed oil, and beeswax can be used to protect and enhance the natural beauty of wood. These finishes are non-toxic and can be reapplied easily as needed.
- **Water-based finishes:** Water-based finishes have low VOC (volatile organic compound) content, making them a healthier and more environmentally friendly option than traditional

solvent-based finishes. They are also easy to clean up with soap and water.

- **Reclaimed wood:** Using reclaimed wood is an excellent way to reduce waste and minimize the environmental impact of woodworking projects. Reclaimed wood can be sourced from old buildings, furniture, or even shipping pallets, and can add unique character and charm to a project.

- **Salvaged hardware:** Instead of buying new hardware, consider salvaging and repurposing old hardware from other projects or items. This reduces waste and gives a unique, vintage look to a project.

- **Upcycling:** Upcycling involves taking old, unwanted items and turning them into something new and useful. For example, old doors can be turned into headboards or tables, and pallets can be transformed into outdoor furniture.

By incorporating these eco-friendly finishes and sustainable techniques into home improvement projects, woodworkers can not only create beautiful and functional pieces but also help reduce waste and protect the environment.

Section 5: The Future of Woodcraft

- Chapter 14: Innovations in Sustainable Woodworking
- Chapter 15: The Intersection of Woodworking and Technology
- Chapter 16: The Role of Woodcraft in Building a Sustainable Future

Chapter 14 : Innovations in Sustainable Woodworking according

As concern for the environment grows, the woodworking industry is increasingly looking for innovative ways to create sustainable and eco-friendly products. In this chapter, we will explore the latest innovations in sustainable woodworking and how they are shaping the future of woodcraft. From new materials to advanced technologies, we will examine the cutting-edge developments that are pushing the boundaries of what is possible in sustainable woodworking. Join us as we take a glimpse into the exciting future of this important craft.

The Latest Innovations in Sustainable Woodworking

Sustainable woodworking has become an increasingly important aspect of the woodcraft industry, as consumers and woodworkers alike recognize the need to reduce the impact of woodcraft on the environment. In recent years, there have been many exciting developments in sustainable woodworking that have made it easier and more efficient than ever to create beautiful and functional woodcraft while minimizing waste and reducing environmental impact.

Sustainable woodworking has become increasingly important in recent years, and as a result, there have been many innovations in the field. Here are some of the latest:

- **Use of reclaimed wood:** One of the most popular sustainable woodworking practices is the use of reclaimed wood. This involves repurposing old wood from buildings, furniture, or other structures for new projects. Not only does this prevent the need to cut down new trees, but it also gives a unique character to the finished product.

- **Use of sustainable forest management:** Many woodworking companies are now practicing sustainable forest management, which involves carefully managing the forests where their wood is sourced. This includes replanting trees after they are harvested, using selective cutting methods to preserve the health of the forest, and reducing waste in the manufacturing process.

- **Development of eco-friendly finishes:** The finishing products used in woodworking can have a significant impact on the environment. However, there are now many eco-friendly finishes available that are made from natural materials and have a lower impact on the environment.

- **Use of alternative materials:** In addition to wood, there are many alternative materials that can be used in woodworking projects. These include bamboo, cork, and even recycled plastic. These materials can have a lower impact on the environment and offer unique properties that make them suitable for different types of projects.

- **Use of technology:** Technology has also played a role in sustainable woodworking, with new tools and equipment designed to minimize waste and improve efficiency. CNC machines, for example, can precisely cut wood and other materials, reducing the amount of waste created.

Overall, these innovations in sustainable woodworking are helping to reduce the impact of woodworking on the environment and promote a more responsible approach to woodworking practices.

How They are Shaping the Future of Woodcraft

The latest innovations in sustainable woodworking are shaping the future of woodcraft by making it more environmentally-friendly and efficient. For example, advancements in technology have allowed for the creation of new materials, such as engineered wood products that use smaller pieces of wood and are more stable than traditional solid wood.

Additionally, sustainable forestry practices are being implemented to ensure that the wood used in woodworking projects is sourced responsibly and does not contribute to deforestation or other environmental issues. This includes certifications and labels that indicate that the wood comes from sustainably managed forests.

Furthermore, advancements in woodworking machinery and tools are making the process more efficient and reducing waste. For example, computer-aided design (CAD) software allows woodworkers to design and plan projects with greater precision, reducing the amount of material wasted due to mistakes or inaccurate measurements.

Finally, eco-friendly finishes and other sustainable techniques are being developed to improve the longevity and sustainability of woodworking projects. These finishes often use natural materials and are free of harmful chemicals that can be harmful to both humans and the environment.

Overall, the latest innovations in sustainable woodworking are shaping the future of woodcraft by promoting responsible and efficient use of resources, reducing waste, and minimizing the impact on the environment.

The Cutting-edge Developments

In recent years, there have been several cutting-edge developments in sustainable woodworking that are pushing the boundaries of what is possible. These innovations range from new materials to advanced technologies and are helping to create a more sustainable and eco-friendly future for woodcraft.

One of the most significant developments is the emergence of new sustainable materials, such as bamboo and reclaimed wood. Bamboo, for example, is a fast-growing and renewable resource that can be used to create a wide range of products, from flooring to furniture. Reclaimed wood, on the other hand, is salvaged from old buildings and structures and can be repurposed to create new and unique pieces of furniture.

Another innovation that is shaping the future of sustainable woodworking is the use of advanced technologies, such as 3D printing and computer-aided design (CAD). These technologies allow woodworkers to create complex and intricate designs with a high degree of accuracy, while also reducing waste and increasing efficiency.

In addition, there has been a growing focus on using sustainable and non-toxic finishes, such as natural oils and waxes, to protect and enhance the natural beauty of wood. These finishes are not only better for the environment, but they also provide a healthier living environment for those who use the finished products.

Overall, these innovations are helping to create a more sustainable and eco-friendly future for woodcraft. As the demand for sustainable products continues to grow, it is likely that we will see even more developments in the field of sustainable woodworking in the coming years.

The Boundaries of what is Possible in Sustainable Woodworking

As sustainable woodworking continues to gain popularity, new and innovative developments are pushing the boundaries of what is possible in this important craft. One of the most exciting areas of innovation is the development of new materials that are more sustainable than traditional hardwoods. For example, bamboo, a fast-growing grass, is an excellent alternative to hardwoods and can be used in a wide range of woodworking projects.

Another exciting development is the use of advanced technologies in woodworking. Computer numerical control (CNC) machines are becoming more affordable and accessible, allowing woodworkers to create precise and intricate designs with ease. 3D printing is also being used to create custom wooden parts and components, reducing waste and increasing efficiency.

Sustainable woodworking is also being influenced by the growing trend of circular economy, which aims to minimize waste and maximize resource efficiency. Woodworkers are exploring new ways to repurpose and reuse waste wood and other materials, creating beautiful and functional pieces while reducing their environmental impact.

In addition, sustainable forestry practices are being further developed and implemented to ensure that the wood used in woodworking projects comes from responsibly managed forests. This includes certification systems that provide consumers with assurance that the wood they are purchasing comes from sustainable sources.

Overall, the future of sustainable woodworking is exciting and full of potential. By embracing new materials, technologies, and sustainable practices, woodworkers can continue to create beautiful and functional pieces while minimizing their impact on the environment.

The Exciting Future of this Important Craft

The future of sustainable woodworking is a bright and exciting one, with new innovations and technologies constantly emerging to help push the boundaries of what is possible. From advances in sustainable materials to the development of new tools and techniques, there are many exciting developments on the horizon.

One area of innovation is the development of new sustainable materials, such as bamboo, which has become increasingly popular as a sustainable alternative to traditional hardwoods. In addition, advances in engineered wood products, such as cross-laminated timber (CLT) and laminated veneer lumber (LVL), offer new possibilities for sustainable construction and furniture making.

Another area of development is the use of advanced technologies, such as computer-aided design (CAD) and computer numerical control (CNC) machines, which can help woodworkers create intricate and precise designs with greater efficiency and accuracy. 3D printing technology is also being explored as a way to create complex wooden structures and components.

Sustainability is also being integrated into woodworking processes, with a focus on reducing waste and maximizing the use of materials. For example, sawdust and wood chips can be converted into biofuels or used for composting, while wood scraps can be repurposed into smaller projects or used as firewood.

Overall, the future of sustainable woodworking is one that is filled with promise and possibility. As technology continues to evolve and new materials and techniques are developed, woodworkers will have more opportunities than ever before to create beautiful and functional pieces while also protecting the environment.

Chapter 15: The Intersection of Woodworking and Technology

As technology continues to evolve at a rapid pace, it has become increasingly intertwined with traditional crafts such as woodworking. From advanced machinery to cutting-edge software, technology is revolutionizing the way we approach woodworking and creating new possibilities for innovation and creativity.

Woodworking has always been a craft that values skill, patience, and a deep understanding of the natural properties of wood. However, in recent years, technology has started to play an increasingly important role in this traditional craft. From computer-aided design (CAD) software to automated machinery, woodworkers today have access to a wide range of tools and technologies that are helping them push the boundaries of what is possible in woodworking.

In this chapter, we will take a closer look at the intersection of woodworking and technology. We will explore some of the latest developments in this field and examine how they are shaping the future of woodcraft. From the use of 3D printing to create custom wood pieces to the development of sophisticated CNC machines that can precisely carve intricate designs, there are many exciting new technologies that are helping woodworkers bring their ideas to life in new and innovative ways.

At the same time, we will also consider some of the potential drawbacks of relying too heavily on technology in woodworking. While these tools can certainly make the process of designing and creating wood pieces more efficient and precise, they can also detract from the unique character and personality that handmade items possess. We will explore these issues and more as we examine the fascinating intersection of woodworking and technology.

The Intersection of Woodworking and Technology

Woodworking and technology have traditionally been seen as two separate fields, but in recent years, the intersection of the two has become increasingly important. Advancements in technology have revolutionized the way we approach woodworking, from design to production, and have opened up new possibilities for creativity and innovation.

One of the most significant ways technology has impacted woodworking is through computer-aided design (CAD) software. This software allows woodworkers to create detailed 3D models of their designs, making it easier to visualize the final product and make adjustments before beginning the actual woodworking process. It also enables precise measurements and calculations, reducing the likelihood of mistakes or errors.

Another way technology has impacted woodworking is through the use of CNC (computer numerical control) machines. These machines use CAD software to precisely cut and shape wood, resulting in more efficient and accurate production. They can also be used to create intricate designs and patterns that would be difficult or impossible to achieve by hand.

3D printing technology has also made its way into woodworking. While not yet widely used in the industry, 3D printing can be used to create intricate designs and prototypes quickly and efficiently.

Virtual and augmented reality (VR/AR) technology is also being integrated into woodworking. These technologies allow woodworkers to visualize their designs in a virtual space, providing a more immersive and interactive experience. They can also be used to train and educate woodworkers, as well as showcase finished products to potential customers.

Overall, the intersection of woodworking and technology is creating exciting opportunities for innovation and creativity. While some traditionalists may be resistant to these changes, the benefits of incorporating technology into woodworking are undeniable.

The Latest Developments in This Field

Here are some of the latest developments at the intersection of woodworking and technology:

- **Computer-Aided Design (CAD):** With CAD software, woodworkers can create digital 3D models of their designs, allowing them to visualize and refine their ideas before ever picking up a tool. This technology also allows for greater precision and accuracy in creating complex shapes and curves.

- **CNC Machines:** CNC (Computer Numerical Control) machines use computer-controlled routers to precisely cut and shape wood according to a digital design. This technology allows for faster and more accurate production, as well as the ability to create intricate designs that would be difficult or impossible to do by hand.

- **3D Printing:** While not yet widely used in woodworking, 3D printing has the potential to revolutionize the industry by allowing for the creation of complex, customized parts and components. This technology could also be used for prototyping and testing designs before committing to a full build.

- **Laser Cutting:** Laser cutters can be used to create intricate designs and patterns on wood, as well as to precisely cut and engrave custom shapes and logos. This technology is particularly useful in creating decorative pieces and signage.

- **Digital Fabrication:** The intersection of woodworking and technology has given rise to the field of digital fabrication, which involves using advanced computer-controlled tools and machinery to create custom products and designs. This technology has the potential to significantly increase efficiency and precision in the woodworking industry.

Overall, the intersection of woodworking and technology offers a range of exciting possibilities for woodworkers, from greater precision and efficiency to the ability to create custom designs and prototypes.

How They are Shaping the Future of Woodcraft

The advancements in technology are shaping the future of woodcraft in numerous ways. One significant aspect is the way technology is being integrated into traditional woodworking processes, allowing for greater precision, efficiency, and customization.

One example of this is the use of Computer-Aided Design (CAD) software in woodworking. CAD software allows woodworkers to create 3D models of their designs and make precise adjustments before even touching a piece of wood. This not only saves time and reduces waste but also allows for greater accuracy in complex designs.

Another example is the use of Computer Numerical Control (CNC) machines in woodworking. These machines use digital instructions to precisely cut and shape wood, allowing for highly intricate designs that would be difficult to achieve by hand. CNC machines also enable woodworkers to produce multiple identical pieces with ease, making mass production of custom designs possible.

Technology is also being used to improve the sustainability of woodworking. For instance, some companies are developing new composite materials made from recycled wood and other sustainable materials, reducing the need for virgin timber.

In addition, digital tools and online platforms are making it easier for woodworkers to connect with customers and showcase their work. Social media and e-commerce platforms allow woodworkers to reach a wider audience and sell their products directly to consumers, bypassing traditional retail channels.

Overall, the intersection of woodworking and technology offers many exciting opportunities for the future of the craft. By leveraging new tools and materials, woodworkers can create innovative designs, streamline their processes, and contribute to a more sustainable industry.

The Potential Drawbacks of Relying too Heavily on Technology in Woodworking

While the advancements in technology have undoubtedly improved many aspects of woodworking, there are also potential drawbacks to relying too heavily on it.

One potential drawback is the loss of traditional woodworking skills and techniques. As more woodworkers turn to automated machinery and computer-aided design, there may be a decline in the hands-on skills that have been passed down through generations.

Another concern is the environmental impact of technological advancements. While some technologies may reduce waste or increase efficiency, they may also require significant energy consumption and contribute to pollution.

Furthermore, reliance on technology may result in a loss of creativity and innovation in the woodworking field. As woodworkers rely more on automated processes and standardized designs, there may be less experimentation and unique designs.

It is important to find a balance between traditional woodworking skills and modern technology to ensure the best possible outcomes in terms of quality, efficiency, and sustainability.

The intersection of woodworking and technology is a fascinating and rapidly evolving field

Certainly! The intersection of woodworking and technology is a fascinating and rapidly evolving field. With the advent of new technologies and the increasing availability of high-tech tools, woodworkers are now able to create complex, intricate designs with greater ease and precision than ever before. From computer-aided design (CAD) software to automated CNC machines, technology is revolutionizing the way woodworkers approach their craft.

However, while there are many benefits to incorporating technology into woodworking, there are also potential drawbacks to consider. Some woodworkers worry that the use of technology may lead to a loss of traditional skills and techniques, or that it may reduce the artistic and creative elements of the craft. Additionally, there are concerns about the environmental impact of high-tech woodworking tools and the potential for increased waste and energy consumption.

Despite these concerns, it is clear that technology will continue to play an increasingly important role in the future of woodcraft. As new tools and techniques are developed, woodworkers will have even more opportunities to push the boundaries of what is possible and create truly innovative and unique works of art.

Chapter 16

The Role of Woodcraft in Building a Sustainable Future

As we move towards a more sustainable future, it is becoming increasingly important to examine the role of traditional crafts in this transformation. Woodcraft, in particular, holds a unique position as a material that is both renewable and versatile. In this chapter, we will explore the ways in which woodcraft can contribute to building a more sustainable future. From using reclaimed and repurposed materials to designing structures and products that are energy-efficient and carbon-neutral, we will examine the many ways in which woodcraft can play a crucial role in sustainable development. Join us as we explore the exciting possibilities of this important craft in the context of a changing world.

The Role of Traditional Crafts in this Transformation

Woodcraft, in particular, holds a unique position as a material that is both renewable and versatile. As we move towards a more sustainable future, it is becoming increasingly important to consider the role that traditional crafts like woodworking can play in this transformation. In this chapter, we will explore the ways in which woodcraft can contribute to building a more sustainable future. From its potential to replace non-renewable materials to its ability to promote local economies and support small-scale production, we will examine the many ways in which woodcraft can help us create a more sustainable world. We will also explore some of the challenges and opportunities facing woodcraft in the 21st century, as well as some of the innovative approaches being taken by woodworkers and designers around the world. Join us as we explore the crucial role of woodcraft in building a sustainable future.

Traditional crafts play a crucial role in building a sustainable future. These crafts are often rooted in centuries-old techniques that have been passed down from generation to generation, and they rely on natural materials and resources that are local and renewable.

By using traditional crafts in sustainable construction and design, we can reduce our reliance on non-renewable materials and minimize our impact on the environment. For example, using locally-sourced wood for furniture or building construction not only reduces transportation emissions but also supports local economies.

Moreover, traditional crafts can also provide an alternative to mass-produced goods that often have a high carbon footprint due to long supply chains and manufacturing processes. Instead, handcrafted items made with sustainable materials can offer unique, high-quality products with a lower environmental impact.

In addition, traditional crafts have the potential to preserve cultural heritage and support local communities. By valuing and supporting traditional crafts, we can promote the continuation of these skills and the preservation of local cultures.

Overall, traditional crafts have an important role to play in the transition to a more sustainable future. They offer a way to connect with our past, create a better future, and promote environmental and social sustainability.

The Ways in which Woodcraft can Contribute to Building a more Sustainable Future

Woodcraft has the potential to contribute significantly to building a more sustainable future. As a renewable material, wood is a key component in the development of sustainable products and building practices. Traditional woodcraft techniques, such as hand carving and joinery, can also play a role in reducing waste and promoting sustainable design.

One way in which woodcraft can contribute to sustainability is through the use of reclaimed wood. This involves salvaging wood from old structures or discarded furniture and repurposing it for new projects. Reclaimed wood not only reduces waste but also adds character and unique features to the finished product.

Another way in which woodcraft can promote sustainability is through the use of local and responsibly sourced wood. By using wood from nearby forests that are managed sustainably, woodworkers can reduce their carbon footprint and support local economies. Certification systems such as the Forest Stewardship Council (FSC) ensure that wood is harvested responsibly and ethically.

Additionally, woodcraft can promote sustainable design by focusing on durability and longevity. By creating well-made, high-quality products that are built to last, woodworkers can reduce the need for frequent replacements and contribute to a circular economy.

Furthermore, traditional woodcraft techniques such as hand carving and joinery require less energy than modern methods, reducing the carbon footprint of the woodworking process. These techniques also often involve less waste and can promote the use of natural finishes and adhesives.

Overall, woodcraft has the potential to contribute significantly to building a more sustainable future. By using reclaimed and responsibly sourced wood, focusing on durability and longevity, and utilizing traditional techniques, woodworkers can promote sustainable practices in their craft and contribute to a more sustainable world.

The many Ways in which Woodcraft can Play a Crucial Role in Sustainable Development

Woodcraft has the potential to play a crucial role in sustainable development by incorporating eco-friendly practices and promoting a more conscious approach to design and production. One way in which woodcraft can contribute to sustainability is through the use of reclaimed and repurposed materials. By salvaging wood from old buildings, furniture, or other sources, woodcrafters can give new life to discarded materials and reduce the demand for new wood products.

In addition, woodcrafters can design structures and products that are energy-efficient and carbon-neutral. For example, wood can be used to create building materials that are both durable and sustainable, such as cross-laminated timber (CLT) and other engineered wood products. These materials can be used to construct energy-efficient buildings that can help reduce greenhouse gas emissions and promote a more sustainable future.

Woodcrafters can also use sustainable forestry practices to ensure that wood is harvested in a responsible and ethical manner. This can involve using selective cutting methods to preserve forests and prevent clear-cutting, as well as ensuring that wood is sourced from well-managed forests that are certified by organizations such as the Forest Stewardship Council (FSC).

Moreover, woodcrafters can also employ eco-friendly finishing techniques, such as using natural oils and waxes, to protect and enhance the natural beauty of wood while minimizing the use of harmful chemicals.

Overall, woodcraft has the potential to contribute to a more sustainable future by promoting the use of renewable materials, reducing waste, and promoting eco-friendly practices. By incorporating sustainable practices into woodcraft, we can help build a better future for ourselves and for generations to come.

The Exciting Possibilities of this Important Craft

Woodcraft has the potential to play a significant role in building a more sustainable future. As we continue to face the challenges of climate change, dwindling natural resources, and a growing population, it is becoming increasingly important to embrace practices and technologies that promote sustainability.

Woodcraft, in particular, holds a unique position as a material that is both renewable and versatile. The use of reclaimed and repurposed wood, for example, can help reduce the need for new resources and divert waste from landfills. Additionally, designing structures and products that are energy-efficient and carbon-neutral can help reduce greenhouse gas emissions and combat climate change.

One exciting possibility for woodcraft in sustainable development is the use of mass timber, which involves using large-scale, prefabricated wood panels and beams to construct buildings. This method is not only more environmentally friendly than traditional construction materials like concrete and steel, but it also offers a range of benefits such as improved energy efficiency, reduced construction time and costs, and increased design flexibility.

Another area where woodcraft can contribute to sustainable development is in the production of furniture and home decor items. By using sustainable wood products and eco-friendly finishes, woodworkers can create beautiful, long-lasting pieces that have a minimal impact on the environment.

In summary, woodcraft has the potential to play a crucial role in building a more sustainable future. By embracing sustainable practices and technologies, woodworkers can help reduce waste, conserve natural resources, and combat climate change. The possibilities for this important craft in the context of a changing world are truly exciting.

Conclusion

- Chapter 17: Taking Action: How to Build a Sustainable Future with Woodcraft

Chapter 17: Taking Action: How to Build a Sustainable Future with Woodcraft

After exploring the various aspects of sustainable woodworking, it's time to put that knowledge into action. In this final chapter, we will provide practical guidance on how to build a sustainable future with woodcraft. From making conscious choices in sourcing materials to designing energy-efficient products, we will discuss the steps you can take to make a positive impact on the environment through your woodworking practices.

We will also discuss the importance of collaboration and community involvement in promoting sustainable woodworking. By working together, we can amplify our impact and create a more sustainable future for generations to come. Whether you're a professional woodworker or a hobbyist, this chapter will provide you with actionable steps and inspiration to make a positive difference through your woodworking practices.

Some Practical Guidance

Building a sustainable future with woodcraft requires a holistic approach that involves sourcing wood responsibly, reducing waste, and choosing eco-friendly techniques and materials. Here are some practical tips to help you get started:

1. **Choose sustainably sourced wood:** Look for wood that is certified by organizations like the

Forest Stewardship Council (FSC) or the Sustainable Forestry Initiative (SFI). These certifications ensure that the wood comes from responsibly managed forests that prioritize biodiversity and protect the rights of indigenous communities.

2. **Reduce waste:** Woodworking can generate a lot of waste, but there are ways to reduce it. For example, you can use wood scraps for smaller projects or turn them into sawdust for use as mulch or fuel. You can also invest in tools and equipment that minimize waste, such as a saw that produces less sawdust or a planer that generates thinner shavings.

3. **Use eco-friendly techniques and materials:** There are many eco-friendly techniques and materials you can use in your woodworking projects. For example, you can use natural finishes like tung oil or beeswax instead of synthetic varnishes. You can also use salvaged or reclaimed wood instead of new wood, or choose composite materials made from recycled wood fibers and plastic.

4. **Consider the entire lifecycle of your project:** From the sourcing of materials to the disposal of waste, consider the entire lifecycle of your project and look for ways to reduce its environmental impact. For example, you can choose to build furniture that is designed to be easily disassembled and recycled at the end of its life.

5. **Educate yourself and others:** Stay informed about the latest developments in sustainable woodworking and share your knowledge with others. Encourage your peers and customers to prioritize sustainability in their woodworking projects as well.

By following these practical tips and adopting a sustainable mindset, you can build a more sustainable future with woodcraft.

The Steps You can take to Make a Positive Impact

Absolutely! As we become more aware of the impact our actions have on the environment, it's important to consider how we can make a positive difference through our woodworking practices. Here are some steps you can take to build a sustainable future with woodcraft:

1. **Choose sustainable materials:** Look for wood that has been sustainably sourced and certified by organizations such as the Forest Stewardship Council (FSC) or the Sustainable Forestry Initiative (SFI). Consider using reclaimed or salvaged wood for your projects, or use alternatives such as bamboo or cork.

2. **Reduce waste:** Design your projects to minimize waste and use every part of the wood you have. Consider repurposing scrap wood for

smaller projects or kindling. Also, ensure that your waste is properly disposed of or recycled.

3. **Energy efficiency:** Design your products with energy efficiency in mind. Consider factors such as weight, insulation, and ventilation to maximize energy efficiency. You can also consider using renewable energy sources such as solar power to power your tools and equipment.

4. **Choose eco-friendly finishes:** Use natural and eco-friendly finishes such as oils, waxes, and shellacs instead of synthetic and toxic finishes. These finishes are often biodegradable and contain no volatile organic compounds (VOCs).

5. **Collaborate with others:** Join a community of like-minded woodworkers to learn and share best practices in sustainable woodworking. Attend workshops and conferences focused on sustainable woodworking to learn from experts and share your own experiences.

By implementing these steps and making conscious choices in your woodworking practices, you can make a positive impact on the environment and contribute to building a sustainable future with woodcraft.

The Importance of Collaboration and Community Involvement

Collaboration and community involvement are key components of promoting sustainable woodworking and building a more sustainable future. Working together, we can amplify our impact and create a more significant change than we could alone.

One way to promote collaboration is to seek out and participate in woodworking communities and organizations that focus on sustainability. These groups can offer valuable resources, information, and support to help you adopt more eco-friendly woodworking practices. Additionally, participating in these communities can help you connect with like-minded individuals, collaborate on projects, and share knowledge and expertise.

Another way to promote collaboration and community involvement is to prioritize local sourcing of materials. By sourcing materials from local suppliers and businesses, you can reduce your carbon footprint, support the local economy, and foster stronger connections within your community.

Finally, involving the community in your woodworking projects can be an excellent way to promote sustainability and inspire others to take action. For example, you could host workshops or classes that teach eco-friendly woodworking techniques, or partner with local schools or community centers to develop sustainable woodworking programs. These efforts can help raise awareness about the importance of sustainable woodworking practices and create a more significant impact in your community.

By working together and involving our communities, we can promote sustainable woodworking practices and create a more sustainable future for generations to come.

www.ingramcontent.com/pod-product-compliance
Lightning Source LLC
Chambersburg PA
CBHW052155220526
45471CB00004B/1691